Know how to live within yourself:
There is in your soul a whole world
Of mysterious and enchanted thoughts...

Fyodor Tyutchev

About the Author

Ellen Dugan, also known as the Garden Witch, is a psychic-clairvoyant who lives in Missouri with her husband and three children. A practicing Witch for over twenty-four years, Ellen received her Master Gardener status through the University of Missouri and her local county extension office. She also teaches classes locally on Witchcraft, magickal herbalism, and practical magick. Look for other articles by Ellen in Llewellyn's annual *Magical Almanac*, *Wicca Almanac*, and *Herbal Almanac*, and the new *Witches' Companion*. Visit her website at:

   www.geocities.com/edugan_gardenwitch

spells to bewitch, bedazzle & beguile

how to
Enchant
a Man

Ellen Dugan

Llewellyn Publications ♥ Woodbury, Minnesota

FIRST EDITION
First Printing, 2008

Book design and editing by Rebecca Zins
Cover design by Lisa Novak
Cover image © Aldis Kotlers/istockphoto
Illustration on page 146 by Llewellyn Art Department

Llewellyn is a registered trademark of Llewellyn Worldwide, Ltd.

Library of Congress Cataloging-in-Publication Data

Dugan, Ellen, 1963–
How to enchant a man : spells to bewitch, bedazzle & beguile /Ellen Dugan. —1st ed.
  p. cm.
Includes bibliographical references and index.
ISBN 978-0-7387-1113-3
1. Witchcraft. 2. Love—Miscellanea. 3. Single women—Miscellanea. I. Title.
BF1572.L6D84 2008
133.4'42—dc22

2007035899

Llewellyn Worldwide does not participate in, endorse, or have any authority or responsibility concerning private business transactions between our authors and the public.

All mail addressed to the author is forwarded but the publisher cannot, unless specifically instructed by the author, give out an address or phone number.

Any Internet references contained in this work are current at publication time, but the publisher cannot guarantee that a specific location will continue to be maintained. Please refer to the publisher's website for links to authors' websites and other sources.

Llewellyn Publications
A Division of Llewellyn Worldwide, Ltd.
2143 Wooddale Drive, Dept. 978-0-7387-1113-3
Woodbury, MN 55125-2989
www.llewellyn.com

Printed in the United States of America

Other Books by Ellen Dugan

Garden Witchery: Magick from the Ground Up
(Llewellyn, 2003)

Elements of Witchcraft: Natural Magick for Teens
(Llewellyn, 2003)

7 Days of Magic: Spells, Charms & Correspondences for the Bewitching Week
(Llewellyn, 2004)

Cottage Witchery: Natural Magick for Hearth and Home
(Llewellyn, 2005)

Autumn Equinox: The Enchantment of Mabon
(Llewellyn, 2005)

The Enchanted Cat: Feline Fascinations, Spells & Magick
(Llewellyn, 2006)

Herb Magic for Beginners: Down-to-Earth Enchantments
(Llewellyn, 2006; also available in Spanish as *Magia con las hierbas*)

Natural Witchery: Intuitive, Personal & Practical Magick
(Llewellyn, 2007)

Contents

contents

Chapter 6 · Bewitching Blossoms, Bedazzling Gems & Beguiling Herbs:
Love Spells, Fascinations & Charms / 117

Chapter 7 • Seasons of Enchantment: Fascinating Folklore and Love Magick for the Year / 145

What Is Enchantment?

So I am lost in your eyes, ears, nose, and throat—
You have enchanted me with a single kiss
Which can never be undone ...

Kenneth Koch

Love is a mystical force and physical presence that moves us throughout our lives and shapes our daily existence in many ways. Think about it for a moment: every woman is either in love, working to keep the flames burning, looking for love, denying that she needs love, recovering from a relationship that has faded, or bemoaning the lack of a good man in her life.

The topic of love magick is a popular one. As well it should be, but not for the reasons you may suspect. Love is the truest, most vital magick I have ever experienced. It is a force of nature, and it is powerful. As a practicing Witch for over twenty-four years, I can tell you without a doubt that magick from the heart is the most potent enchantment I know of.

Sure, the title of this book, *How to Enchant a Man*, may have grabbed your attention, and you are excited and very curious. But now that I have your interest, let's really think about this for a moment. What do you believe I am really implying when I use the word *enchant*? Do you suppose I am just using a play on words? Or is *enchantment* simply a clever metaphor for attraction? Could *enchant* be used to describe an emotional state instead? And as long as we're on a roll ... just what *does* the word *enchant* mean, anyway?

According to my handy-dandy *Webster's New Collegiate Dictionary*, the word *enchant* is defined as the following:

> 1. To sing to. 2. To influence by or as if by charms and incantation;
> bewitch. 3. To attract and move deeply; rouse to ecstatic admiration.

This classic definition lays the groundwork for explaining the practice of Witchcraft and magick. In the old days, to enchant something was to sing to it—yes, literally to sing a rhyming charm over it—which would be another way of bewitching something.

Today, the word *Witch* also has several popular implications. Some folks envision the classic, scary-looking Halloween-type of witch (you know, the old crone who cackles over a cauldron). They may imagine a beautiful, seductive fictional character from the movies, television, and popular fiction, or they may know the truth. Let's be clear and take a moment to brush away the hype and lies, and take a look at the reality of actual magick and real Witches.

A Witch is a magickal practitioner, male or female, and/or a follower of an earth religion, such as Wicca. Wicca is a legally recognized religion here in the United States, and Wicca is a quiet, loving, and peaceful path. Wiccans vow to harm none with their magick, and they follow a strict code of nonmanipulation—which, in case you were wondering, is the type of magick you are going to find in this book.

Will it be fun? Of course. Will you truly be able to perform these spells and charms all by yourself? Absolutely. And I bet you really want to ask ... *does the magick really work?* You betcha!

Now, for those of you who are new to the practice of Witchcraft (also referred to as the Craft), you will need to understand how this all works and to be familiarized with the mechanics of magick. And those of you who are experienced practitioners know exactly why.

In this "how to" book, you will find techniques to help you pull the energy of love and romance into your life. There will be spells and charms as well as a discussion of the rules when it comes to magick and love. Yes, rules. There is no such thing as a free lunch, and you need to understand the rules of the magickal game so you don't get burned.

The Magick of Love

Love is the magician that pulls man out of his own hat.

Ben Hecht

Love is not unlike magick, as they are both something that must be experienced to be truly understood. Since understanding these mysteries only comes after the experience, you have to get in the trenches and enthusiastically live your life. The easiest way to fall in love is to be in love with life. The secret to attracting others is to feel and to believe that you are attractive and worthy of love yourself. Love begins when you take pleasure in everyday activities. So I invite you to look around and to experience your world as a Witch does. Discover the enchantment that is inherent in all of nature and in all beings.

By the time you finish this book, not only will you know how to enchant a man, you also will have discovered how to work with the positive, natural, magickal forces that are all around you to bring joy, happiness, and enchantment into your life. *Bon voyage!*

Chapter 1

Enchantment Is a Woman's Bewitching Art

Those fingers in my hair
That sly come-hither stare
Leaves my conscience bare
It's witchcraft.

Carolyn Leigh & Cy Coleman, "Witchcraft"

My favorite way of explaining to people what magick is and how it works is to use the following analogy. I find that it is effortless to visualize and easy to understand. So if you have read my books before, this will seem familiar to you. If not, I think you will find these next few paragraphs particularly helpful. So settle in, get comfortable, and get ready to learn.

Magick is the art and science of creating positive change in your life. Magick is also a force of nature that is as yet unexplained by science. In truth, all of nature is interconnected, not unlike the filaments of a spider's web. Have you ever gently touched the outside edge of a spider's web? The slightest touch or even a breeze will cause the web to tremble. So begin to envision the cosmic world and your environment as a spiritual web. Here, each and every one of the world's religions are woven within its strands, for all of creation and nature is interconnected, one to the other. A belief in and the practice of positive magick is one of the ways of being connected to this web of life. As we perform magick and cast our loving spells to bring about a positive change, we are, in actual fact, gently weaving new patterns into that spiritual web.

Magick is a sympathetic process. It works on the basis of your own personal psychic power and a connection, vibration, or harmony between things. Magick revolves around the essence of life, the power of the four natural elements of earth, air, fire, and water, and a reverence for the natural world. This respect for the life force and empathy with the forces of nature are at the very heart of all magickal practice.

The use of spells and magick is not a New Age fad. It is, in fact, an ancient practice. Chances are you have already felt the power of magick or even have cast a beguiling spell or two before and weren't even aware of it. If you wear perfume, you have tapped into the power of scent to shift your mood and to make yourself seem more attractive for a special someone. There is also the romantic tradition of the language of flowers. Flowers and spicy, floral scents have a deep and rich history of mythology and folklore. When it comes to love, most folks know the basic floral meanings, especially when it comes to one of the most popular types of flowers to give to a lover, the rose.

Traditionally, red roses are associated with desire and passion, while pink roses are associated with romantic love. White roses symbolize a pure, innocent love, which is how they became so popular as bridal flowers. Have you ever received a bouquet of roses from a man and wondered why they work so darn well, to either soften you up after an argument or to let you know his intentions? It's because you too have fallen under the spell cast by the giver of the flowers and of the blossoms' magick, folklore, and history. *Hmm,* you're wondering . . . *can magick truly be that simple?*

Yes, it can.

However, magick is a paradox. It is beautifully simple, but it is also complex. It can be as gentle as being showered in rose petals or as dangerous as being struck by a bolt of lightning. Too scary of a comparison for you? Well, I am being honest here. I'd much rather have you be blissfully covered in rose petals than be painfully burned.

Rules of the Game

You can't practice Witchcraft
while you look down your nose at it.

Aunt Jet, Practical Magic

When it comes to magick and love spells, there are a few rules that you need to follow. By keeping these rules in mind and allowing them to guide your enchantments, you will ensure that your magick is nonmanipulative and positive. Magick can certainly be used to enhance your appearance, to bolster your confidence, to improve your attitude,

enchantment is a woman's bewitching art

to catch a fellow's attention, and to sweeten up your outlook on life, which then makes you more attractive.

However, enchantments should not be used to force or coerce someone or manipulate their emotions. If you cross the line and break the rules, you will find yourself dealing with consequences in ways you never could have imagined. A woman who understands the rules of enchantment knows that her role is to attract, to select a partner, and then to love. No matter how tempted you may be to pursue, snag, and bag the guy, magick is not a weapon to be used for a man hunt.

The spells featured in this book should contain your best and most positive personal energies. They should carry the mental image of the kind of love you wish for. Spells and enchantments do have the power to bring real change into your life. Spells and charms do indeed work, and as they manifest, they take on a force and energy of their own. This spell-created energy literally brings life to the result you desire. Keeping this in mind, let's take a look at the rules of enchantments and ethical Witchcraft.

> **Harm None.** Let me be absolutely clear: harm *nothing*. Not yourself, not other people, not animals or plants. Do not damage someone's property or the environment. Magick is about joy, love, and creating positive change; it is not about stirring up trouble, taking from another, or causing chaos, pain, or anger in any way. You should work your spells and charms for the best possible outcome of the situation for everyone involved—which is yet another way of making damn sure that the spell you are casting will cause no harm.

Manipulation Is Bad. Never work any magick that's going to influence the free will of another. Now, you can certainly work an enchantment to attract a lover in general, but never cast a spell to entrap a specific someone. Only an unbalanced or unwise woman would resort to manipulative magick to get a man. A man who doesn't want you of his own volition is not the right man for you. Would you like someone to take away your right to choose who *you* fall in love with, or to falsely manipulate your emotions or feelings? I didn't think so. Considering this aspect of magick denotes a mature individual, and this is where your personal ethics and sense of honor come into play. It is important to honor the sacredness of love and to have respect both for men and for yourself. This is the key to ethical magick.

Do Not Target Anyone Specifically. This is a very important point and worth hammering home one more time. When you work your spells and charms, ask for the "correct person for you," not a specific individual. Sure, Mr. Studly Corporate Guy from work may seem like every girl's dream . . . but he could end up being your own personal ultra-conservative, conceited, stuffed-shirt nightmare. You never know, the nice mechanic who fixed your transmission might end up being the lover and romantic partner of your dreams. The best romantic relationships are the ones that surprise you! Because when it comes to love, you just never know. So do not put limitations on the spellwork or on yourself. Let things unfold, and see what happens.

enchantment is a woman's bewitching art

♥

Respect the Tides of Nature and the Elements. Magick springs from all these sources. The spells and charms in this book will work together with the seasons, cycles and phases of the moon, and the four natural elements of earth, air, fire, and water. When you work as one with nature, your spells and charms flow better and are much more effective. You will find a more detailed description of the magick of the elements and the tides of nature, and how this power can be incorporated into loving enchantments, in chapter 4.

Celebrate Your Connection to the Goddess. Goddess is the deity to call on when you are dealing with magick that involves love and attraction. The Goddess is a kind and loving deity, and she is also a triple deity, meaning she has three distinct aspects to her persona. She is the strong and independent Maiden, the loving and comforting Mother, and the wise old Crone. She comes from every culture, all over the world, and has many different names, personalities, and specialties. Sometimes she is simply referred to as the "Great Mother" or "the Lady." In this book, you will be introduced to several different aspects of the Goddess. But no matter how you envision her, if you are sincere and have an open heart, she will hear your magickal request, and she will answer you. Romance is one of the Lady's specialties.

Follow the Rule of Three. There is a traditional rule to Witchcraft and magick that states, "Ever mind the rule of three, three times what thou givest returns to thee." This means whatever type of magickal energy you send out with a spell, be it positive or negative, will circle around and return straight back to you—

amplified three times over. So it only makes sense to keep your enchantments in an affirmative, nonmanipulative, and loving tone. Bottom line: magick is a lesson in cause and effect.

Love Magick Can Be Unpredictable
How to Avoid Being Burned

Love must be as much a light as it is a flame.

Henry David Thoreau

Well, jeez! you may be thinking... *I only wanted the spells!* Well, guess what? You are getting so much more. It would be irresponsible, not to mention careless, of me to just fill up this book with mysterious-sounding spells and then leave you hanging, completely unaware of what will happen when you abuse magick and dabble in the Craft. To have success with your spells, you will need to behave responsibly, to believe in the magick, and to follow its rules.

Now before you start to roll your eyes at me (I have teenagers who roll their eyes at me every day, thank you *very* much), I'd like to tell you why it is so important not to target anyone specifically when you work love-themed enchantments. No, I am not taking away all your fun; I am expecting you to act like an adult. These rules are important for you to follow, because they can save you from a world of problems later on. Not convinced? Here are a few examples of what can happen if you ignore the rules when it comes to love and magick.

Typically, when you work a manipulative love spell on someone specific, all hell breaks loose. When the spell takes hold, the target of the spell often becomes emotionally unbalanced, and in fact he or she becomes a victim of the spellcaster's manipulation. This happens for several reasons. First, some part of the victim instinctively knows that something is wrong, and they try to fight it. On an intuitive level, they sense that something different is happening, and their whole system struggles to rid itself of the unwanted energy. Now, if the victim of the love spell has any type of psychic talent, they will experience a manipulative love spell as a sort of psychic attack. (Classically, a psychic attack happens when someone else's unwanted energy attaches itself to another person.)

The victim may initially be attracted to you as the caster of the manipulative spell, but they do not know why, nor do they understand what is happening to them. So they may act out, become hostile toward you, or behave completely differently than what you had expected or could have ever possibly imagined.

Also, there is an excellent chance that the unwilling target of a love spell will become obsessive with the caster. This could blow your image of the adoring, devoted love slave right out of the water. Sure, it's fun and even satisfying to imagine a man pandering to your every whim for a while … but then reality sets in. That kind of groveling behavior gets old very quickly. I have heard many war stories about this type of spellwork over the years, and all the tales end badly. Typically, the target of the love spell will sulk, start to become angry and increasingly aggressive, and then become completely obsessive if you are out of their sight for any length of time. Gee, where's the fun now?

Or things may totally backfire, and the spellcaster themselves may be the one who becomes obsessive. I know of one individual who became so obsessed with the object of her love spells that her whole world imploded. She tried everything, including manipulative spells, to keep her ex-lover. She knew better than to target someone specific. It didn't matter to her that they had broken up or that he was seeing other women. Many people tried to reason with her, but alas—she was too caught up in her own drama, and she refused to let him go.

She rationalized the manipulative love spells by saying their love was meant to be. It had to be, and she all but smothered him. Even though he tried to stay friendly, he soon sensed something was wrong and became frightened of her and her obsession. Eventually he got a restraining order against her. Was that enough for her? Did she finally cease and desist? Unfortunately, no.

This ex-couple worked in the same office, and one day she spotted him with his new lady in the company lunchroom. She created such a nasty scene that she was put on unpaid leave, escorted from her place of employment by security, and told not to return without a written recommendation from a psychiatrist.

I think we can safely label this a way *not* to enchant a man. So no, I'm not trying to sound like your mother with all these warnings and rules. I am instead giving you the rules to magick so you can understand the reasoning behind them. Remember that loving enchantments seek to create a positive change for the good of all. Now that you understand the rules and ways of magick, you will be able to make intelligent, wise, and informed decisions.

Getting Started

Find the Magick All Around You

> Well, there is magic all around you, if I do say so myself,
> I have known this much longer than I've known you.
>
> *Stevie Nicks & Rick Nowels, "Rooms on Fire"*

If your goal and intention is to bring love into your life, then putting yourself in the correct frame of mind is the best way to start. To employ spells and charms and incorporate the Craft into your life is to be aware of your connection with every thing in the universe. Remember the spiritual web we discussed before? Working magick taps into the natural energy that is all around you and directs it out into your life for a specific purpose. I think Laurie Cabot says it best, in her book *Love Magic*: "Magic is the ability to alter one's state of consciousness at will in order to effect some change in the world."

To succeed at magick, you have to work at it. Yes, there are the magickal accesso- ls, and the spell verses that are employed. However, there is also a mental and nergy needed to catalyze the spell. This mind energy is the same energy that web of life. When you release this personal, intuitive, and magickal energy, t in all directions through the universe.

A vital part of enchantment is learning to act on your intuition. When was the last time you honored your feminine intuition? Intuition is actually a spontaneous "knowing" described as an insight, or an inner voice. It is also a precognitive experience, meaning that you are receiving information about future events, people, and places. Intuition is more than a "hunch." This is information that is gathered from your soul.

What do you suppose would happen if you tuned in and paid attention to your instincts and let your intuition guide you when it comes to romance and love? Well, for starters, you could get a better sense of the men that you meet. Pay attention to your inner voice and see what it tells you about the new people you come across. Do not deny or invalidate your Goddess-given powers. If you block this out, you are closing the door on your awareness to other enchanting realms of magick. By embracing your feminine intuition, you also can tap into your magick easily.

To begin, simply quiet your mind and listen to that inner voice. Pay attention to your physical reactions, too. If your stomach tightens painfully, then your intuition is warning you: so proceed with caution. If you get a little stomach flip or a pleasantly warm-feeling rush, your intuition is giving you a heads-up. The type of man you are looking for may be found more easily when you combine enchantment with your own feminine intuition. Your instinct could literally help you be in the right place at the right time. Try it for yourself, and start believing in your own abilities.

Within your grasp, there is a vast array of magickal talents and psychic abilities. They are not mysterious or otherworldly, they are natural—as natural as the earth you stand on and the moon and sun up in the sky. Allow these psychic experiences into your life. Open up to the possibilities of working in harmony with your feminine intuition, for

enchantment is a woman's bewitching art

we can only experience what we are willing to acknowledge. Truly, there is a Witch in every woman.

Witchy Woman

Witchy woman, see how high she flies
Witchy woman, she got the moon in her eye.

Don Henley & B. Leadon, "Witchy Woman"

A Witch does not hunt for love; instead, she attracts it and draws it to her. A clever Witch allows nature to take its course. There is an old saying in the Craft that calls for practitioners to "follow their bliss." This means that you should focus on yourself and make yourself joyful and content first. If you can do that, men will be drawn to you of their own free will.

The truth is, if you want to enchant a man, first you need to be enchanted with yourself and happy in your own life. How many of you have noticed when you are feeling lonely and desperate for a relationship that a good man is nowhere to be found? But the minute you are in a happy and stable relationship, available men seem to pop up all over the darn place—which is enough to make you want to smack your hand to your forehead and wonder where they were hiding all this time. Honestly, they weren't hiding at all.

Men are typically attracted to a happy, confident woman. Men are enchanted and fascinated by feminine verve, strength, energy, and confidence. Also, in a man's mind there is something captivating about a strong woman who desires him but doesn't really need him. It drives him crazy, but deep down he finds that irresistible.

There is an unstoppable power to a confident and balanced woman. There are such fabulous and positive magickal qualities to being an enchanting woman; a few of these are strength, love, a sense of nurturing, a capacity to heal and to soothe with voice and touch, and of course we have a finely developed intuition. As women, we tend to give away too much of our power and self-worth worrying about our bodies instead of working with what we do have. The spells and techniques in this book will help you learn to play up your best assets and give you plenty of ideas on how you can tap into your own enchanting abilities. Women who are confident in themselves and who embrace their own unique feminine qualities are sensual, glowing, and creative—and are by their very nature magnetic.

Become a Love Magnet

I believe that there is a subtle magnetism in Nature,
which, if we unconsciously yield to it, will direct us aright.

Henry David Thoreau

Now we move on to the physical rules of attraction. The spells and charms that you are about to work can be successfully used to send out your individual and enchanting personal energy. This will, in turn, help to attract the correct lover for you. With a little magickal know-how, you can indeed make yourself more desirable and magnetic.

enchantment is a woman's bewitching art

When a woman is magnetic, she possesses an extraordinary power to pull in and to attract. To attract what, you wonder? Why, whatever she most wants and is willing to work towards, my dear. This can be a positive change, a new man in her life, prosperity, knowledge, protection, a promotion … whatever she most desires.

All women are magnetic. It is a gift from the Goddess. A Witch simply taps into this natural power and shapes it with purpose, then directs it out into her life. This receptive and enchanting power can be tapped into quite easily. These are natural forces at work here. As discussed before, magick works *with* the energies of nature, not against them. Magnetism is a physical phenomenon. This phenomenon involves a science that deals with fields of force, or energy (as in one that is attracted to another). Magnetism is also defined as the ability to attract or to charm. If someone is "charmed," they have been affected by magick. They are gently compelled, delighted, and drawn to you of their own free will. They are attracted.

This, then, leads us neatly to a discussion on receptive power. To be receptive is to be able to receive, to draw in, to be open and responsive. Receptive power is inherently feminine. Also, you have to realize that receptive power is not weak or submissive. Oh, no. Receptive power is magnetic, compelling, and fascinating.

Magnetism happens when there is a polarity of energy. One way to think about this is to realize that projective masculine energies and receptive feminine energies are in a continuous cosmic dance. This compelling action between these two powers is a true force of nature. To be receptive is to be open to all the enchanting possibilities that are out there and then to pull this in towards yourself. If you want a crash course in how to draw in energy, take a deep breath in. When you inhale air, you can feel the power of drawing in.

So envision yourself as a captivating individual who has the power to draw in and to attract that which she most desires. See yourself as a beautiful and bewitching woman, because that is exactly what you are! Open up your soul and allow more fun, spontaneity, joy, and beauty into your life. Act like a goddess. For when you allow that inner magickal light to shine, you have to put aside old, preconceived ideas and images of yourself and are, in fact, allowing the essence of love and enchantment to come into your life.

Enchanting Workspace
The Love Altar

Each cloud-capt mountain is a holy altar;
An organ breathes in every grove;
And the full heart's a Psalter,
Rich in deep hymn of gratitude and love.

Thomas Hood

A good way to begin your enchantments is to craft an altar. This will be a magickal workspace in which to create these future loving and positive changes that you are bringing into your life. Most people think that an altar is something that's only found in a church or a temple. But you can certainly create your own personal, magickal altar

enchantment is a woman's bewitching art

in your own house. This is a simple and elegant way to invite the sacred and the divine into your life every day.

Having a sacred space specifically for you to work your enchantments is a wonderful way to reinforce your positive intentions. Now keep in mind that your magickal workspace can be any shape or size, and it ought to reflect your own personal taste. It should be decorated and styled in a way that makes you comfortable and happy. Elaborate and theatrical or simple and modest—it's your call. So start looking around your place and figure out just what handy surface could be transformed into a suitable altar.

You could use a television tray and make your altar portable and temporary. Or you can use an end table or the top of your dresser and keep your working space as a permanent setup. It's completely up to you. Your altar will help you stay connected to the Goddess, and it will help remind you to stop and to experience the loving magick that is found in your life. Your goals and desires for change are going to be represented on this magickal workspace, so take the time to select items for it that are important and special to you.

Remember to keep this working altar as a place of reverence. Do not sit mundane items on it, such as dirty dishes, keys, or the mail. Keep it a separate and special place devoted just to your magick. Also, don't be afraid to change things around occasionally or to switch them out. Try different colors and keep your altar looking fresh, pretty, and inviting.

To give you a few ideas for setting up your love altar, try the following items. To cover the work surface, I would use a red or rosy pink (whichever color you prefer)

24- to 36-inch square of natural fabric. For fabric you can use cotton muslin, or you can go all out and cover the surface with a silk scarf. Use natural fabrics, as they are more complementary to the energies of magick and enchantment.

Place a nice photo of yourself on this altar; after all, this is magick for you, and you will need something to represent yourself. Also, you should add a little magnet, to represent the feminine power that you posses to "pull in" and to attract. Now, to add a little witchy atmosphere to your altar, I would add some soft lighting. For illuminator candles, a couple of plain white taper candles in holders are perfect. Please note that if candles are not an option for you, then use a small and decorative lamp with a low-wattage bulb.

Fresh and fragrant flowers in a vase are always a wonderful addition, as well as a few natural representations of each of the four magickal elements. Try a pretty stone or a crystal cluster for the element of earth; a feather to symbolize the element of air; a seashell for the element of water; and a small red candle or a lava rock to signify the element of fire. If you like, you may add a small statue or a framed picture of a goddess to your altar setup as well. Sprinkle fresh flower petals or star-shaped confetti on the altar to jazz things up. Add a dish of spicy potpourri, or burn some of your favorite romantic incense. Be creative, and see what you can conjure up!

Now that you have your love altar set up and ready to go, here is a simple spell to consecrate it and to make the workspace ready for your future spells, charms, and enchantments.

enchantment is a woman's bewitching art

♥

Consecrating the Love Altar

Set up the altar to your personal preference. Refer to the previous suggestions for ideas. Then, once you have things arranged to your liking, light your illuminator candles, tap the table four times (once for each element), and say the following consecration charm:

Elements four, gather around at the sound of my voice,
Bringing dreams and hopes to reality; this is my choice.
I do consecrate and bless this loving altar today,
May it draw blessings and joy, in the best possible way.
By the powers of earth, air, fire, and water,
I create positive change, fun, love, and laughter!

Now take a moment and enjoy the love altar that you have created. You could meditate for a while or just sit back and enjoy the beautiful atmosphere. When you are finished, extinguish the illuminator candles and know that your love altar is all ready and waiting for you to begin casting your first spells and charms. You have just laid the groundwork for love to come into your life.

Love Spells: A Primer

She held me spellbound in the night
Dancing shadows and firelight...

Don Henley & B. Leadon, "Witchy Woman"

ow, on to the stuff you've been waiting for: the spells. For those of you who are new to the idea of enchantments and magick, and who are gleefully plotting out the first thing you'll do ... let's start out by discussing what a spell truly is. A spell is a conscious, formal attempt to direct magickal power and energy to achieve your personal goal. I have also seen a spell described as a well-thought-out wish that carries with it the power to come true. The simplest way to explain this is by giving you a basic definition of the word *spell*. And it goes a little something like this ...

A spell is a series of rhyming words that verbally announces the spellcaster's intention. When these spoken words are combined with specific actions, such as lighting a candle, creating an amulet, or gathering an herb, this is then worked in harmony with the tides of nature. Combined with the spellcaster's personal energy, this endows the magickal act with the power to create positive change.

But no matter how you look at the word *spell*—whether it is a basic description of the word or a careful definition of the act—magick is a fundamental part and force of nature. It is found everywhere, in the simplest of things: flowers, colors, stones, herbs, the very earth itself. And it is possible to learn how to harness this energy and to use it successfully.

Now, the love spell is probably one of the most popular requests when it comes to magick. However, as we've discussed in the previous chapter, magickal emotional manipulation is *way* out of bounds for the ethical Witch. And you know why ethics are important: Witchcraft is called the Craft of the Wise. This is where your own personal wisdom comes into play. Just how smart are you, anyway? Are you smart enough to use magick ethically and for the best of all those involved? Ah, now you see why we went over the rules of magick right off the bat. There is so much more to love magick than just the "you shall be mine" type of fictional love spell.

You can, in fact, revitalize passion in a loving relationship or improve your personal appearance, thereby making yourself more noticeable and enchanting. You can ethically work inner and outer beauty spells, draw a loving relationship into your life, work on communication between you and your partner, and add a little spice to a physical relationship that seems to have lost its zing. These scenarios and many more are possible.

The sky is the limit, and remember that affirmative actions create a blissful result and a positive reality.

Believe and Receive
The Art of Spellcrafting

If you believe in magic, come along with me
We'll dance until morning till there's just you and me
And maybe, if the music is right
I'll meet you tomorrow sort of late at night ...

Joe Sebastian, "Do You Believe in Magic?"

Yes indeed, there is an art to crafting a spell. But it is simpler and more instinctual than you are probably imagining. To begin, you have to believe and then allow yourself to receive. Just like that old song from the 1960s, you have to believe in magick. Spellwork is easier to do and will garner better results if you truly believe in what you are doing. Doubt and second-guessing yourself will squash any chance for the spell to work. You have to believe in a spell to bring it to life. There will be a few "warm up" spells at the end of this chapter for you to work, and they will help you to build up that magickal confidence. When you try your hand at those simple spells for self-improvement, you will begin to see the outcome of your work—allow yourself to receive the benefits. Your confidence will grow and your successes will become more obvious. You simply have to believe and to know down in your heart that the enchanting possibilities are endless, and then allow those delightful results room to grow.

There is an old Witch's rule that teaches a spellcaster the following adage: To know, to dare, to will, and to be silent. This is called the Witch's Pyramid. It is, in essence, the very building block of magick and enchantment. While this saying seems deceptively simple, if you take a look at its principles you will begin to comprehend why much of magick and the Craft is about determination, personal strength, and an ethical way of living your life.

When we take this phrase apart, piece by piece, and look at each of the four challenges, the significance becomes much more apparent. Here we go:

To know means to know yourself. Who are you? What are your goals? What sort of loving and compassionate person are you? *Know thyself* was inscribed on an ancient temple at Delphi. This is an elegant way of reminding you that to be balanced and ethical you need to have yourself together emotionally. Be sure to know exactly what it is you are casting for.

To dare means that you have courage; you are daring to study the magickal arts and working to create a positive change. Working spells and enchantments is a leap of faith. You have to have a certain amount of daring to try to manifest these wonderful changes in your life. Honestly, magick is for bold and daring individuals. In this second step, you are daring to be wise.

To will means to express resolve and to be unwavering. You are "willing" these positive and loving changes into your life with your magick, so you must have the determination to succeed, plus the strength to live your life as a caring and ethical person. This is the test of your personal strength, of your will and inner determination to bring loving, positive change into your world, because the sheer force of your will is the magick of intention. Now, just to keep things interesting, the only difference between *intention* and *will* is the amount of space you give magick the chance to play out. Don't try to control the outcome. Instead, relax and believe in the work you have done. This third step is all about having faith in your own personal power and then being strong enough to allow the magick to blossom on its own.

To be silent is fairly self-explanatory. Silence is the foundation that the other principles are built upon. It is also the hardest to achieve. The final step in spellcasting calls for you to sit tight and allow the spell to manifest in its own way. Don't think the process of magick to death, and keep quiet about the spellwork you perform. Why? Because spells are intimate, very personal things. If you nervously blab to your girlfriends that you have worked a romance-drawing spell, for example, this creates disbelief with your friends, and it may generate some negativity or jealousy. All that type of negative energy really kills that spark of hope and the careful energy of your spellwork. The more you talk about the spell, the more energy you are draining away from it. So zip your lips, don't worry it to death, and allow the magick to unfold. Be confident.

love spells: a primer

♥

There is an old saying in the Craft: "Do a spell, and then forget about it." What this means is to work your enchantment and let it unfold while believing in your magick. You know the spell will succeed because you dared to have the will to make the positive change. You have to be confident and open-minded to let the magick run its natural course. If you sit and worry over the magick, you are holding in the spell. Let it be free, and let it make the positive change that you have envisioned.

Remember to be receptive to, and to leave space for, all the possibilities and positive outcomes to manifest. Bottom line: if you truly believe in the magick and in yourself, you will receive the outcome you are working toward.

Magickal Supplies and Tools of the Trade

Every girl's got to have her supplies … and it may surprise you to learn the supplies used in the Craft are much less dramatic than you might expect. As magick springs from nature, our supplies are easy for you to find. You probably have many of the required spell ingredients around your house, such as candles and herbs. For the most part, the ingredients you will require will be natural items: stones and crystals, a feather, a shell, various herbs and flowers. So, no worries. This isn't going to cost you a fortune. Magick works with nature, and it links into the subtle energies that are inherent in the simplest of natural items.

Candles and Conjuring

How far that little candle throws his beams!

Shakespeare, Merchant of Venice

Now on to a favored supply in magick and enchantments: candles. Candles are a standard tool employed for just about any type of enchantment. The fantastic thing about candle magick is that it quickly and neatly combines the magick of color, light, and scent. Traditionally, candles have been lit to welcome the divine and to symbolize our connection with the powers of light and color. The act of lighting a spell candle is one of sacredness that then radiates out to illuminate the rest of your day.

The spell candle is a traditional symbol of the power of the fire element. Especially for our purposes, this magickal element is an excellent one to tap into, as fire brings us the qualities of warmth, heat, and illumination (all of which can certainly be worked into your loving enchantments). Candle spells are a classic part of any Witch's repertoire. Why? Because a burning spell candle is a physical representation of the actual spell. As long as the candle burns, it is shining your enchanting energies out into the world.

To get your candle spells really up and moving, you will want to use the correct color. Color has a powerful influence on our moods and in our living environment. In the Craft, colors are important components to magick as well. Each shade has their own unique enchanting correspondences and uses. Now in the following list, these colors all revolve around the theme of this book: loving enchantments. While working candle magick I urge you to always keep your candles attended, and to think safety first.

love spells: a primer

♥

Please burn your candles safely and in their appropriate holders, and keep the flames clear of flammable items, children, or curious pets.

As to the shape or size of the spell candle, well, that's completely up to you. You may use a votive, a taper, a pillar, a mini spell candle, or a tealight. Personally, I like to work my candle spells with votive candles because they are inexpensive, come in a vast array of colors and scents, burn for approximately six to eight hours, and can be picked up anywhere. That way, it's easy to keep a nice assortment of colors and scents on hand.

Also have a little package of plain white tealights readily available. These unscented, plain candles come in handy for all sorts of magick. Tealights are practical and very affordable, they are already in a little cup, you can float them in water if you want to, and they burn for approximately three to four hours. I have yet to meet a Witch who didn't have a stash of plain tealights. Trust me, you will use these babies all the time.

Tips and Tricks for Candle Magick

Here are a few more little tips about votive candles, candle magick, and safety in general. These Witch's tips will come in handy for you, so read them over before you dive right into candle magick.

Witch's Tip #1: A good rule of thumb when it comes to candle magick is to remember that you should work only one spell per candle; it keeps the intent purer. Let the candle burn until it's completely gone. (Just keep an eye on it. Never leave burning candles unattended.)

Witch's Tip #2: If you use votive candles for your spells, remember that they turn to liquid right away as they burn. So always burn votive candles inside votive holders. Otherwise, you'll have a puddle of wax all over your work area.

Witch's Tip #3: For easy removal of any leftover wax after the votive burns out, try this: before you light the candle, put a teaspoon of water in the bottom of the votive holder, place the candle on top of it, then light the candle. As the candle starts to burn and then melt, that water creates an air pocket, and when the candle is spent, you can easily pop any leftover wax right out of the holder.

Witch's Tip #4: A good all-purpose candle color is white. If you do not have the specific color of candle that a spell calls for, you can easily use a white candle instead. The white candle will work out beautifully, and this is a no muss, no fuss alternative.

Witch's Tip #5: The color chart listed on the next page is a basic color inventory. Purple, for example, can range in hues from the softest lilac to the deepest amethyst; however, the magickal definition will remain basically the same. A good rule of thumb to follow in color magick is this: the paler the color, the gentler the magick; the deeper the color, the more intense the magick.

love spells: a primer

♥

And finally, here is a rainbow of colors to incorporate into your loving enchantments. Explore the following color chart, and let's get that creativity flowing!

Color Chart for Loving Candle Spells

Pink: Affection, friendship, charm, a first love.

Red: Love, desire, passion, magnetism, the Goddess as a Mother, and the element of fire.

Orange: Sexuality, energy, verve, and improving concentration.

Yellow: Charisma, mental powers, communication, creativity, and the element of air.

Green: Prosperity, health, good luck, fertility, and the element of earth.

Blue: Hope, peace, emotion, love, healing a broken heart, intuition, and the element of water.

Purple: Psychic powers, spirituality, and increasing personal power.

Silver: Goddess magick, serenity, elegance, wisdom.

Gold: The God, the sun, success, abundance.

White: All-purpose color, the moon, clarification, the Goddess as a Maiden.

Black: Release, to end relationships, protection, the Goddess as a Crone.

Adding a Touch of Aromatherapy to Your Candle Spells

But, soft! methinks I scent the morning air …

Shakespeare, Hamlet

You didn't think I'd leave you hanging with that comment on scented candles, did you? Nah, I've got you covered. For those of you who also enjoy scented candles, here is a quick rundown of some of the common votive candle scents and colors you may find—and how to incorporate these into your enchantments. In this correspondence chart, the scent is listed first, followed by the color of the candle in parentheses. After that is the magick best suited to the color and scent combination. In keeping with our topic, they all revolve around the theme of love and romance.

Apple scent (red): Love, health, and healing a broken heart.

Blueberry scent (blue): Protecting a relationship, personal protection, and healing a lover's spat.

Cinnamon scent (brown or red): Passion, energy, prosperity, and love.

Citrus scent (yellow or orange): Clearing away old hurt feelings, and promoting fresh beginnings.

Gardenia scent (white / off-white): This old-fashioned scent brings about love, peace, and healing.

Lavender scent (purple): Cleansing, removing old, stale ideas and emotions, and encouraging protection.

Lilac scent (purple): For a first love, encourages the favor of the faerie kingdom and protects a true love. Lilac is also a powerful cleansing scent. Use it when you feel that you have been exposed to jealousy or negativity.

Patchouli scent (black): There are many uses for patchouli. It can be a sexually stimulating scent, and it can also be used with the color black for protection. In this color-scent combo, use it to end an unhealthy relationship, to break a love spell gone sour, and for banishings.

Pine scent (dark green): Brings the power and richness of the earth element. This encourages fertility, prosperity, and healthy relationships.

Pumpkin / spice scent (orange): This scent promotes happy homes, family love, and a sense of bounty and prosperity. It's a good scent to celebrate the bounty that love has brought into your life.

Rose / floral scent (pink): Innocent love, flirtation, romance, encouraging new friendships. This soothing scent and soft color also helps to heal a broken friendship.

Rose scent (red): The classic love spell combination. This brings love, romance, sensuality, and passion.

Sandalwood scent (white): For spirituality and sex. It also increases your personal power.

Vanilla scent (off-white): Traditionally, this scent is a Kitchen Witch's old trick to encourage love and desire in men (do you remember your grandmother dabbing vanilla extract behind her ears?). Also, vanilla scents can be used to celebrate the comfort of love and to promote a loving home environment.

A Simple Scented Candle Spell
Finding Your Inner Goddess

Here is a simple little self-confidence spell for you to try your hand at. This one will help you get those magickal juices flowing, and you can work this whenever you want to, at any day or time. Plus, I am sure you are getting impatient to try your hand at a spell or two, so here we go. This spell helps you remove any negative thoughts about yourself or any internal denigration you may have been carrying around. We talked about this in the first chapter, remember? Hit that *mute* button on self-criticism. You are a Goddess, a bewitching and enchanting woman. So let's start acting like one!

All you need for this spell is a white votive candle, a coordinating votive holder, a picture of yourself (you can use the photo that's currently on your love altar), and a lighter or matches. Go ahead and set up this spell on your altar. If you'd like to employ a bit of magickal aromatherapy while you're at it, you may use a vanilla-scented candle or simply add a drop of vanilla extract to the candle before you light it. (Yes, the stuff that you bake with. It's in your kitchen cupboard. I told you we'd be using simple and natural things from around the house!) We are going with the scent of vanilla, as it is used to celebrate love and is a comforting scent, which is just the ticket for this spell.

Light your illuminator candles. Then set the vanilla candle in its holder. If your candle is unscented, add a drop of vanilla extract to the top of the candle. Now set the picture of yourself in front of that candle holder. I want you to picture yourself happy, confident, and successful. See yourself glowing with confidence and joy.

Close your eyes and picture a little spark deep down, inside your heart. Now coax it up to a nice, bright flame. Now light the vanilla candle, place your hands over your heart (where that inner spark is shining), and repeat this verse three times:

As the scent of vanilla wafts around,
No more self-doubt or sadness will be found.
As this candle burns away, let my inner light shine,
I see myself for who I am: a Goddess divine!

Close the spell with these lines:

For the good of all, causing harm to none,
By fire's bright magick, this spell is done!

Allow the candle to burn until it goes out on its own. If you wish, this spell can be repeated as often as you like—once a day or once a week, whenever you feel like you need a boost to your self-confidence.

There is something haunting in the light of the moon;
it has all the dispassionateness of a disembodied soul,
and something of its inconceivable mystery.

Joseph Conrad

If you work your magick with the cycles of nature instead of against them, your spells and enchantments will unfold more smoothly. A powerful aspect of spellwork to be considered is moon magick, including the moon's phases and cycles and the daily astrological correspondences.

For a magickal practitioner, tapping into lunar energy is a simple and profound way to add more power to your loving enchantments and charms. The moon is associated with the Goddess and with women's mysteries. As mentioned in the first chapter, the Goddess is a triple deity; there are three distinct features to her personality. She is seen as the Maiden, the Mother, and the wise old Crone, and each of these aspects corresponds to a specific lunar phase.

The Maiden is linked to the waxing moon, the slim crescent that we see in the evening sky. It looks like a smile in the west, just after sunset. As the nights pass, the moon grows in shape and is higher in the sky. The Mother aspect of the Goddess is connected to the full moon, which rises in the east at sunset. The Crone corresponds to the waning moon. The waning moon rises later in the evening and slowly shrinks back to a crescent moon, with its points facing down toward the earth.

If you are new to magick, the lunar terms of *waxing* and *waning* may throw you off. Just think of it this way: as the moon waxes, it grows fuller and brighter each night. As it wanes, it becomes less round and smaller and darker. Below you will find the definitions of the three major phases of the moon, the Goddess energy, and the loving enchantments that will correspond with each phase. If you are wondering how you will know what phase the moon is currently in, I suggest that you consult the Internet, your local paper, or any magickal or lunar calendar for the information, and then make your magickal plans accordingly.

> ***Waxing Moon:*** (From new to full, first to second quarter.) Associated with the Maiden Goddess, this is a phase of beginnings, a time of growth and for building up magickal energy. Cast spells now to enhance your appearance and for mystery, enticement, and attraction. As the moon grows fuller each night, this phase is used to pull positive changes toward you.

> ***Full Moon:*** (The full moon phase lasts for three days: the night before the full moon, the day of, and the night after.) The full moon is associated with the Mother aspect of the Goddess. The full moon is an all-purpose lunar phase, and as you'd expect, it is the most powerful. Spells for attraction, fertility, and manifestation are best worked in this phase. Also, spells and charms for passion, power, love, and life are complementary. This is a time of celebration, magick, and thankfulness.

Waning Moon: (From the day after the full moon to the dark of the moon—the third and the fourth lunar phases.) As the moon becomes smaller in the evening sky, this time of the waning moon is associated with the Goddess as the wise, compassionate Crone. This is the phase when it is best to look inside yourself and release old perceptions, banish old ideas and bad habits, or gently dissolve relationships that you have outgrown. Cast your spells now to push away, to release, or to banish problems in your life.

Full Moon Tealight Candle Spell
For Beauty and Joy

I promised a few simple spells for you to practice with, so here you go! This spell needs to be worked on the night of the full moon. This way, you are taking advantage of a powerful magickal time to jump-start this spell. The supplies that you need are uncomplicated and practical.

Please note: tealight candles take approximately four hours to burn. You may work this spell inside, on your love altar, or outside. Just make sure if you cast this spell outdoors that you bring the candle back inside so you can keep an eye on it until it safely burns out.

Supplies

- 1 plain white tealight candle in its metal cup

- 1 small terra-cotta saucer or a small fireproof plate

- A 2 x 2-inch slip of paper and a pen

- Lighter or matches

- A view of the full moon

Directions

Set this up in a place where you can see the full moon; if possible, allow the moonlight to filter down on your love altar/workspace. On the slip of paper write the following: "Allow beauty and joy to fill my life." Then add your initials to the paper. Fold up the little paper and lift the tealight out of its cup. Place the slip of paper in the bottom of the tealight cup. Set the tealight back in the cup, right on top of the little slip of folded paper.

Next, place the tealight inside of the saucer, and give yourself a few moments to center your thoughts. Allow all the strains and troubles of the day to simply drain away from you. Once you feel centered, take a deep breath in and blow it out slowly.

Now tip up your face to the light of the full moon and whisper a sincere greeting to the Goddess. Try saying something like "Hello, Lady Moon" or "Hello, Mother"—whatever you feel inspired to say in greeting is just fine. Then light the candle, and repeat the spell verse three times:

Little tealight candle, burning warm and bright,
Lend your magick to me on this full moon night.
May I walk in beauty each and every day
Bring joy to my life in the best possible way.

Close up this full moon candle spell with these lines:

By all the power of three times three,
As I will it, then so shall it be.

Allow the candle to burn in a safe place until it goes out on its own. If necessary, pick up the saucer and move the spell candle indoors. Once the tealight has burned out, you will notice that the candle wax has sealed your little slip of paper to the bottom of the candle cup. Your spell is sealed and working away. You may now neatly dispose of the leftover metal cup in the garbage. Put away the rest of your supplies, and clean up. Keep your eyes open and watch for beauty and joy to manifest in your life. Pay attention, and notice how the moon has an influence on your life and your womanly intuition and emotions.

Days of the Witch's Week
The Daily Correspondences

> See golden days, fruitful of golden deeds,
> With joy and love triumphing.
>
> *John Milton*

Oh, I can just hear you ... fretting because you missed the recent full moon! You may be panicking because perhaps you need a waxing moon, and we are currently in a waning moon phase (or vice versa). So, if you don't want to wait a few weeks for the moon to be in the correct phase, what in the world do you do?

You go with what you've got. Instead of the moon, you can focus on the seven bewitching days of the week. There's a lot of magick that is found in each and every one of those days, Sunday through Saturday.

Now that you have a handle on the phases of the moon and its magick, let's take the next step forward and study the daily correspondences as well. This is the next step in your lessons on loving enchantments. Eventually, you will be able to combine all of this information as you create your own personalized spells, charms, and rituals. As mentioned earlier, each day of the bewitching week is ruled by a different planet. Every individual day of the week has its own astrological and magickal correspondences, and even its own specialties when it comes to loving enchantments.

The trick is to tap into them and to learn to use these daily magicks in your favor. Where there is a Witch, there is always a way. For example, Monday is the day of the week that is dedicated to the moon and to women's magick. (Which means that in a pinch, the tealight spell we just did could be worked on any Monday, as it's the

chapter 2

♥

38

moon's day, or even a Friday, the day that corresponds to the planet Venus, to encourage beauty.) See, this gives you many more spellcasting options.

For those of us who don't want to wait a few weeks for the moon to be in whatever phase, a Monday would work out just fantastic for a lunar-themed enchantment. The same thing also holds true if you need to remove a problem situation or person from your life, like an old boyfriend who refuses to move on. You don't have to wait for a waning moon, you could work the spell on a Saturday, the day of the week to work magick for releasing old relationships, removing negativity, and banishing problems.

So, without further ado, here are the daily magickal correspondences. What makes this list unique is that it is aligned to the topics and themes of love, attraction, desire, and romance. Read these over carefully, and take your time to absorb the information. You will find the planets, symbols, Goddess information, colors, herbal, and other daily information very useful in your spellwork. Also, the next time you are wondering what sort of spells you could perform on any given day of the week, you'll be able to know at a glance. For a more in-depth look at each of the days of the Witch's week and their magick, spells, and charms, please refer to my book *7 Days of Magic*.

Daily Enchantments for Love and Romance

And all my days are trances
And all my nightly dreams
Are where thy dark eye glances
And where thy footstep gleams...

Edgar Allan Poe

love spells: a primer

♥

Sunday

Work spells on this day for success, recognition, winning, blessings, fitness, and fame. Sundays are all about success, personal accomplishments, and feeling good about who you are. If you are starting a diet, a healthier way of living, or a new exercise program, Sunday is the day to jump-start your goals with a bit of powerfully triumphant solar magick.

Astrological / planetary influence: Sun

Planetary symbol: ☉

Goddess: Brigit, Celtic goddess of inspiration, light, and fire

Candle colors: Yellow and gold (yellow to help with self-expression and for sunshine and healing energy; gold for fame, victory, riches, and success)

Herbs and flowers: Angelica, calendula, sunflower, carnation, and marigold

Foods and spices: Orange and cinnamon

Crystals, stones, and metals: Carnelian, diamond, amber, tiger's-eye, quartz crystal, and gold

Monday

Work spells on this day for women's mysteries, lunar magick, controlling your emotions, improving intuition, to add a sense of mystery to your persona, and for glamours. A glamour is a sort of magickal boost to your appearance. (We will go over glamours in more detail in chapter 6.)

Astrological / planetary influence: Moon

Planetary symbol: ☽

Goddess: Selene, Greco-Roman goddess of enchantment, the moon, and magick

Candle colors: White, silver, and pale blue for a bit of feminine serenity and the moon's mysteries. These shimmery and lunar colors are perfect for any spells on a mystical and moony Monday.

Herbs and flowers: Jasmine, mallow, wintergreen, moonflower, white rose, and gardenia

Foods and spices: Melons, coconut, and mint

Crystals, stones, and metals: Moonstone, pearl, and silver

Tuesday

Tuesday is considered a masculine-energy type of day. Work spells today for passion, sex, seduction, courage, energy, and the strength to fight for what you believe in. If you need to invoke some feistiness into your life, Tuesday is the day. Also FYI: if you want to cast a sizzling spell to encourage some crazy, hot sex between you and your lover, call on Lilith, she won't let you down. Tuesday night may become your favorite night of the week!

Astrological/planetary influence: Mars

Planetary symbol: ♂

Goddess: Lilith, a Sumerian goddess (Lilith is a winged goddess of seduction)

Candle colors: Here we have a feisty and strong combination of magickal colors to choose from: red (for passion), black (for the darker side of love), and orange (for energy; you're going to need it).

Herbs and flowers: Nettle, holly, thistle, anemone, snapdragon, and yucca

Foods and spices: Garlic, allspice, pepper, and ginger

Crystals, stones, and metals: Bloodstone, garnet, ruby, and iron

Wednesday

Work spells for versatility, communication, wit and wisdom, movement, good luck, and to speed things up! And if you need to shake things up, meet new people, and get things moving forward, Wednesday is the day.

Astrological/planetary influence: Mercury

Planetary symbol: ☿

Goddess: Iris, Greco-Roman messenger goddess of the rainbow and communication (Iris is the female counterpart of Mercury, the winged foot messenger of the gods)

Candle colors: Purple and orange are traditional for the planet Mercury, or you could use a rainbow-colored candle for Iris

Herbs and flowers: Iris, fern, lavender, and lily of the valley

Foods and spices: Almonds, beans, dill, and parsley

Crystals, stones, and metals: Opal, agate, aventurine, and quicksilver

Thursday

Work spells on Thursday to attain your long-term goals, encourage prosperity, bring a sense of confidence, and lend an aura of extravagance and royalty to your appearance. Thursday is also a good day to boost your confidence and to celebrate the richness and bounty of a loving relationship.

Astrological/planetary influence: Jupiter

Planetary symbol: ♃

Goddess: Juno Moneta, the Roman mother goddess

Candle colors: Both green and royal blue are associated with Jupiter; use these for prosperity, confidence, and royalty

Herbs and flowers: Oak leaves, dandelion, honeysuckle, lily, hyssop, and meadowsweet

Foods and spices: Sage, cloves, and nutmeg

Crystals, stones, and metals: Sapphire, amethyst, turquoise, and tin

Cast your spells for friendship and happiness on a Friday. Spells for attraction, love, beauty, fertility, luxury, romance, and pleasure all are harmonious with Friday energy. Friday is the big day for romance and sweet, loving seduction.

Astrological/planetary influence: Venus

Planetary symbol: ♀

Goddess: Freya and Aphrodite/Venus. Freya was the Norse goddess of Witchcraft, love, and magick, and Friday was named after her. Aphrodite was the Greek version of the Roman Venus. Aphrodite/Venus is venerated as a Goddess of beauty, love, and sexuality.

Candle colors: Pink and aqua are traditional for the planet Venus. Plus, pink is a soft, romantic color, and aqua brings to mind the color of the sea that Aphrodite/Venus sprang from when she was born.

Herbs and flowers: Catnip, tansy, violet, feverfew, lilac, geranium, roses, and tulip

Foods and spices: Apricot, apple, strawberry, sugar cane, tomato, thyme, and vanilla

Crystals, stones, and metals: Rose quartz

Saturday

Cast your spells on a Saturday to remove obstacles, for protection, to gently but firmly end relationships, or to banish problems. I should also mention here that Saturday is also the day to break any spells that didn't pan out the way you expected. But since you are smart enough to think before you cast and not use manipulation, I doubt that will be an issue.

Astrological/planetary influence: Saturn

Planetary symbol: ♄

Goddess: Hecate, Greco-Roman goddess of the crossroads, transformation, and magick

Candle colors: Black and dark purple are both associated with Saturn, and they are both powerful and protective magickal colors

Herbs and flowers: Ivy, mullein, lobelia, hellebore, morning glory, and pansy

Foods and spices: Beets, quince, and pomegranate

Crystals, stones, and metals: Obsidian, hematite, jet, and lead

Correspondence Charts
Where There's a Witch, There's a Way

There be none of beauty's daughters
With a magic like thee;
And like music on the waters
Is thy sweet voice to me.

Lord Byron

Correspondence charts do come in very handy for magick, because all the corresponding, or complementary, magickal items are listed for you in a straightforward manner. These charts quickly show you what items will work together well. It also allows you to assemble the components for your spellwork with a minimum of fuss. Correspondence charts are great reference materials to have. I'll bet you will refer back to this particular daily magickal correspondence chart quite often, for when you understand the energy and magick that each day of the week and the cycles of the moon hold, you become beautifully in tune with nature and her magick.

So, now that you have a working knowledge of the basics, let's move on to another bewitching topic. I have no doubts that you will find this next chapter absolutely *charming*.

Chapter 3

Charmed, I'm Sure: Attracting a New Love

I see her in the dewy flowers,
I see her sweet and fair:
I hear her in the tuneful birds,
I hear her charm the air.

Robert Burns

As I began this chapter, I turned to an old, reliable source of information: the dictionary. Sometimes you need to get back to basics and look at the word and its essential meanings. As I flipped through *Webster's New Collegiate Dictionary* and the *American Heritage Dictionary* to read the various definitions of the word *charm*, I found them to be most illuminating. Read the following descriptions and consider them carefully.

Charm: *(verb)* 1. To affect by or as if by magick: an act that has or expression believed to have magick power; compel. 2. To please, soothe, or delight by compelling attraction. *(intr.)* 1. The chanting or reciting of a magick spell. 2. A trait that fascinates, allures, or delights. 3. To practice magic; an enchantment.

In the first chapters, we discussed a very important concept in ethical love and romance magick: a Witch attracts and draws what she desires toward her—she doesn't chase a man. This compelling and very natural energy is an offshoot of personal magnetism, which we discussed in the previous chapter.

What we are working toward here is to make you so alluring, so captivating, that your selected potential romantic partner becomes very attracted to you *all on his own.* You will be delighting him by working your unique, personal mojo. In other words, he will be completely fascinated by your personality and appearance, and so entranced by the overall package, that he freely pursues you.

So, yes, he will be affected by magick. A woman's subtle and most powerful witchery, that natural ability that all women possess, is the ability to charm.

You know what charm is: a way of getting the answer *yes*
without having asked any clear question.

Albert Camus

Flirting is a form of human interaction that usually expresses romantic interest in another person. Flirting can consist of conversation, body language, or brief physical contact. It is used as a way to express an interest in another person and to smoothly test the waters to discover if the other person is interested in courtship.

Charm is an important element in flirting. When you add charm to flirting, it wins over even the toughest and most successful men. And any woman can flirt. (Actually, two-thirds of all courtships are initiated by women.) With flirtation, one size fits all. You can be shy or outgoing; it doesn't matter. What matters is that you posses a hint of desire and a sparkle of fun in your eyes.

This process begins with just being friendly. Being open and approachable invites people to come closer. A woman who has mastered the art of flirtation will be confident and secure in herself. You should enjoy introducing yourself to others. Be warm, be friendly, and exude charm. Men are attracted to a friendly smile, a touch of humor, and a woman who is confident enough to look them straight in the eye when she is speaking to them.

It is recommended that you keep your eye contact to just a moment or so. Otherwise, extended eye contact is seen as a sign of aggression or of intense emotion. So make eye contact when you are introducing yourself, hold it for a moment, smile, and then break eye contact. You don't have to be ultra aggressive; you can totally catch a man off-guard if you are just your charming self. If you are being introduced or are introducing yourself, flash a friendly smile and offer your hand in a nice handshake.

You can practice your romantic flirting by working on your social flirting. The way you treat people in your day-to-day life is a great way to exercise those flirting skills. Flirtation is a kindness, a compliment, and a social skill; flirting is not a sexual maneuver. With any type of flirting, you want to make the other person feel great about themselves. And you, in turn, become more approachable.

There is a power in being a woman and in being feminine. At its most basic level, it makes men feel more manly. Being feminine is not a derogatory term. You can still be empowered, sexy, gracious, witty, and friendly *and* be an empowered woman. All people are drawn to those who smile, laugh, have a good sense of humor, and are personable and upbeat. It makes you stand out. You become interesting and bewitching. When you flirt, you are, in fact, working to fascinate the other person with your charm and personality.

You should be very selective as to your choice of flirting target. Flirt with intention as opposed to flirting for the hell of it, which is another way of reminding you to harm none and to avoid manipulation. If you only flirt when you mean it, and with kindness instead of calculation, you will notice a big difference in men's reactions. Overall, they will be much more positive.

The art of flirting is designed to bring out your own fascinating qualities and to let them sparkle so that others can then be drawn to you of their own interest and free will. When people first meet you, their initial impression of you is based upon your appearance and body language. In fact, over half of their overall impression is based on this alone. Next on this list is your style of speaking, which covers a third of their impressions of you. Lastly, only a smidgen of what you actually had to say is figured into their overall impression, so making a good first impression is critical.

Flirting takes the ordinary and makes it extraordinary. It is an art of subtle confidence. Remember that flirting is a way of connecting from the heart and acknowledging someone that you'd like to have the opportunity to know. Be kind, be generous, and have a little innocent fun!

Flirting 101

I'll sing to her, each spring to her
And long for the day when I'll cling to her
Bewitched, bothered, and bewildered am I ...

Lorenz Hart, "Bewitched, Bothered and Bewildered"

Flirting is mostly nonverbal. It's wearing that killer outfit that makes you feel powerful and sexy. It's that lingering glance across a room, a hand drawn through soft, fragrant hair, an alluring smile ... These are subtle witcheries, and they are made up of psychological, verbal, and sensual components. Here are the top flirting techniques. Feel free to apply these in different scenarios, as warranted by the occasion. Just remember to take your time and to keep the pace slow. Don't scare off your potential romantic partner by coming on too strong or too fast. Let them wonder about you.

charmed, I'm sure: attracting a new love

♥

These flirtations start out pretty mildly. They range from suggestions on your personal appearance to the initial contact. As the list continues, the degree of flirting gets taken up to a more serious and intense level. These flirting techniques run the gamut from "Here I am!" to "Don't you wish you had me?" to "Come and get me, big guy!"

Wear high heels. Find a pair of comfortable and flattering heels, and wear them. They are flattering to the legs, and men love high heels. They also make you walk completely differently than if you were bopping around wearing tennis shoes. You will move more deliberately in heels, a bit slower. It's just one of those mysteries of life, but women do feel taller, sexier, and more powerful in a great pair of shoes—and men do notice.

Show a little leg. Wear a skirt or a dress that shows off your legs. It doesn't have to be super short or have a slit up to the mid-thigh to be sexy. Go for alluring and classy. Wear the style and length of skirt that you feel great in.

Wear lipstick. A painted mouth is a sexy mouth. Whether you go for pale honey tones or deep, dark red, lipstick draws attention to your mouth, and there is something about a painted mouth that just yanks a guy's chain. This subtle witchery makes you more alluring, and it announces "Here I am" and "Don't you wish you had me?" all at the same time.

Paint your fingernails. Whether you have long nails or short, trim them up and paint them. If you have shorter nails, try painting them in a soft, sheer nude color. It makes your fingernails look clean and pretty, and your hands will look elegant and attractive. If you feel more daring, paint those nails a deep red or even darker shades of burgundy, violet, or plum. (Please, no chipped fingernail polish. It's *so* tacky! Take the time to freshen up that manicure before you go out.) Also, moisturize your hands. Nope, not kidding. Make the skin smooth and soft. This way, when you gesture with your hands, he notices that you take good care of yourself.

Wear black. It's always in style and it's sexy, mysterious, and slimming!

Wear a shade of red. If you can pull off a bright siren-red dress, suit, or sweater, go for it! Bright red too much for you? Then wear deeper shades of red, from crimson to burgundy. How about deep pink? If the shade flatters your complexion and coloring, try it. The deep pink shade will get you noticed.

Don't sit with other women all night. Most men are probably not going to approach you if you are gabbing away in a pack of gals. Circulate the room and look for an opportunity to introduce yourself.

Repeated, brief eye contact. The "I see you; do you see me?" Look again a few moments later, and check to see if he's looking back.

Smile! (You'd be surprised how often we overlook this one!)

Eye contact and a smile. This is for the "Hey, he *is* looking!" moments. Now that you have his attention, look at him again, meet his eyes, and smile.

Look over your shoulder and smile. This is a classic signal that you are interested in him. It also looks glamorous and fantastic. So as you circulate around, turn and toss him a slow smile over your shoulder.

Get up, go over, and introduce yourself. With a smile and with confidence. You can't just sit there and hope he'll work his way over. What are you, a Victorian heroine out of a romance novel or something? Get out there, girl!

Pay a compliment, receive a smile. Now that you have introduced yourself, try a compliment: "I love that tie" or "You have the most interesting eye color"—that sort of thing. Be kind, and be charming.

Light banter, exchanging compliments. This usually occurs right after the introductory compliment and smiling at each other stage.

Watch your language. Sure, we all lose our tempers from time to time and let rip a vocabulary with colorful expletives—however, when it comes to enchanting a man, I doubt you're going to captivate him by swearing like a sailor.

Whisper. It draws them in closer.

Wink. A saucy little wink, a toss of the head, and you've definitely got his attention.

Play with your hair. Your hair is your crowning glory, and it is an often-overlooked tool for flirting. Run your hand gently down your hair or slowly tuck a bit behind your ear. The key words here are *gentle* and *slow*. Make the movements luxurious, as if you have all the time in the world. You want to snag their attention, not make them flinch out of the way because you are throwing your hair around like you're in a shampoo commercial.

Cross your legs. Arch your back gently and cross your legs high. Then slowly run your hand down your thigh for a moment. Now check for his reaction. This maneuver falls into the "Don't you wish you had me?" category.

Look him over from head to toe, nod with approval, and then smile at him. This one falls into the "Come and get me" category.

Lick your lips, slowly. Yes, this falls into the "Come and get me" category, too. If you are purposefully doing this, then you are going to scramble his brains. So make sure this is what—and who—you want *before* you toss this overtly sexual flirtation his way.

Touch. Last, but not least, we come to "the touch." This can be performed in varying degrees, from a slight touch on his arm while you are speaking to running your hand down the lapel of his suit or trailing a fingertip down his arm while keeping eye contact. (Now you know why it's important to have your hands looking nice—if you touch him, he's going to look down at your hands.) In the flirting stage, I recommend that you keep your touch brief, limit your touching to his arm or shoulder, and keep the mood light, playful, and friendly.

Charm and Courtship

Courtship flirting is the demure, feminine science
of sweetly attracting a man
until he falls madly and inescapably in love.

Ronda Rich, What Southern Women Know About Flirting

In today's world, we move into the physical side of a relationship at warp speed, which can ruin the chance for a long-term relationship. You want to entice a man and fascinate him first. Be a little mysterious ... don't give it all away too fast. I'm not suggesting that you tease the guy to the point of explosion or hold out forever, but I'd sure as hell make him work for it. Aren't you worth a little extra effort? Men love the thrill of the chase and the intrigue of the pursuit. A little anticipation is good for the soul. It's just human nature to want something more, especially if men have to woo, wait, and work for it.

Remember that dating men tend to think along the lines of hunt, explore, chase, and capture. If you give up all the goods right away, so to speak, where is the challenge? Where is the excitement? There is no mystery there, and he's probably going to be bored quickly and move along to the next woman. So once you have his attention and courtship has begun, how do you keep him interested until you are sure he is worthy of your heart and your body?

Well, keep being your enchanting self, and give the relationship time to blossom. If he is worthy of you, he won't mind waiting a little. You can even let him think the courtship, wooing, and waiting section of the program is all his idea. Men need to feel in control, and they like to take charge of any situation. (Whether or not they can depends on the individual.) However, a wise woman lets him think he's making all the moves. She guides her partner along gently, sweetly, with good humor and with love. Usually, a well-besotted man is too happy to notice that he's not the one actually in charge—he just thinks he is, Goddess bless him.

Having a strong sense of self-esteem is a crucial factor when you are working your charm, because once you have snagged a man's interest, there needs to be more. Looks and attraction won't take you past initial contact. Once a man has returned your attention and the "let's get to know each other better" phase has begun, you will in turn need to up the ante, so to speak. How do you do that? You start by giving them your full attention, allowing your own unique personality to truly shine through, and by being your fascinating little self.

This is called the courtship phase, and don't overlook it or hurry past it. Courtship has a magick all its own. In the section that follows, you'll find a few bewitching ideas to get things moving or to keep things interesting while you are in the courtship/dating phase of the relationship. Now is the time to play up what you naturally have and use it to your advantage. In chapter one, we talked about self-esteem and finding the Goddess within. Here is where you'll put that to practical use.

Fascination

What It Is and How to Work It

There's a line between love and fascination

that's hard to see on an evening such as this.

Ned Washington, "My Foolish Heart"

The classic meaning of *fascination* is the power to transfix another and to hold them spellbound by an irresistible power. This traditional definition does, however, make many conscientious practitioners of the Craft cringe. *Aaaack! Did she say "spellbound"? What about free will? What about nonmanipulation? What about harming none?* I can hear some of you hyperventilating right about now. Okay, time out. Do you need to breathe slowly in a paper bag, or are you pulling yourself together? Let's take a deep breath here, calm down, and behave like grownups.

In reality, when I speak of fascination I am speaking along the lines of commanding someone's interest or the ability to be irresistibly charming. To fascinate a man is to capture his whole attention—and to keep his attention wholly focused on you. That is the essence of fascination . . . and wouldn't that come in handy during the courtship phase of any relationship? Why, absolutely.

Interested? I thought you might be. Here are some ideas for fascination, and for these all you need is yourself, your personal magnetism, and maybe a few accessories that I'll bet you already own. Now, when it comes to the accessories, I can just picture you imagining all sorts of exotic and magickal ingredients.

Would you believe me if I told you that you are more likely to find these enchanting accessories in your dresser drawer or closet? I am not speaking of Witchcraft tools and supplies here. No, ma'am. I am speaking of a more practical type of magick, a woman's magick. For example: great lipstick, a damn good bra, a pair of very sexy shoes, an enchanting personal scent. Some of these suggestions we touched on in the flirting section, and others we haven't talked about at all. So let's take a closer look at what tools are readily available to you in your enchanting arsenal of women's natural magick . . . and then let's get to work.

Hair

Gimme a head with hair,
Long beautiful hair,
Shining, gleaming,
Streaming, flaxen, waxen . . .

Gerome Ragni & James Rado, Hair

Our hair plays a significant role in first impressions. Why else would our whole day be ruined when we are having a bad hair day? Your hair is your crowning glory, and it is an enchanting accessory, no doubt about it. Your hair frames your face and body. It tells others about your femininity, sexuality, and personality.

For centuries, people have assigned certain personality traits to specific colors of hair. Whether you agree with it or not, it is true that these generalized traits do add to men's overall impressions of you.

Traditionally, a brunette was supposed to be earthy, alluring, and sexy. From amber-colored hair to chocolate brown, the many shades of brunette pack quite a visual punch.

Blond hair, in its many shades and golden hues, is romantic and dazzling. Blonds are thought to be either movie-star glamorous with platinum hair, or sweet and virginal with light blond-colored tresses.

Redheads are considered flamboyant, with red-hot tempers and ever-changing moods. These dangerous creatures can be innocent and shy with bright red tresses, or they are considered seductive flame-haired sirens with deep red bewitching hair.

Women with black hair are thought to be exotic, mysterious, and mystical, while women with silver hair are considered mature and in possession of an inner wisdom (not unlike the Crone aspect of the Goddess, the wise woman).

Now, when it comes to your personal hairstyle, there is even more information to add to your overall image. It is interesting to note that when men look at women with short, tousled hair, to them, that style conveys confidence and an outgoing personality. Short, sleek hairstyles are thought of as confident, kicky, and sexy, while medium-length hair often suggests an aura of romance and a relaxed woman who has intelligence and a warmth about them. Long hair can send out vastly different messages. If it is long and unstyled, it suggests that the woman is old fashioned, very conservative, or prim. Long, disheveled hair can portray a free spirit or a nature lover; it may also, sadly, make you appear unkempt. Pulling your hair back, off the face, actually conveys intelligence. And if that long hair is styled with accessories, in braids, or in a fancy updo, then we have a different message altogether. Having long hair that is stylish, healthy, and shiny projects sexuality and wealth.

What sort of message do you think you are sending out about your hair? Whether you agree or disagree with this information, the bottom line is that your hair does draw attention to your face—so consider carefully what message you send out with your personal hairstyle. At its best, your hair can reflect your personality and frame your face to its best, most enchanting advantage. It can draw the eye to your throat and neck . . . and it also draws a man's eye down to the cleavage.

The Décolletage

Self-confidence is a powerful beauty-potion.

Nancy Collins

Speaking of cleavage, how do you feel about yours? Do you work with what you have, or do you moan and groan, worrying that you don't have enough or fretting that you think you have too much? Back in chapter 1, where we talked about finding your inner Goddess, I encouraged you to stop beating yourself up emotionally about your own body. And I meant it. Here is where you can put that advice into practice. So take a deep breath, stand up straight, and honey, go with what you've got.

Be clever and be merciless when playing up this part of your anatomy. It's a fact of life that men like breasts. It's something about the caveman days and men being attracted to a woman with full breasts and a rounded backside. This told the primitive man that this female was fertile and had a good chance of successfully bearing offspring. (Seriously. No, I didn't make that up. I'm only passing on the information.)

Truthfully, I don't care how old you are, every woman deserves a decent and a flattering bra. Try satin in deep red or lace in black. There is a rainbow of colors out there in every size. Nobody has to wear a plain, white cotton bra—unless they want to. So, put those puppies in an attractive harness and work 'em!

No matter what bra size you are, A cup or double D, I suggest going out and investing in a few good bras. If you are not sure what size you wear, or feel like your current bra doesn't fit properly, then go to the lingerie department and have a saleswoman fit you in a bra. This is no time to be embarrassed. For those of you who imagine that you're going to be fitted by an old, whisper-voiced matron, you may want to brace yourself.

I recently purchased a very sexy black lace bra and was unsure if I needed to go down or up a size when the young salesgirl knocked on the fitting-room door.

"How's it going?" she asked cheerfully.

I have what my grandmother would term a "generous bustline," so finding a sexy, comfortable bra is always a challenge. "Um, I'm not sure," I answered hesitantly.

Well, before I could say anything else, she unlocked the fitting-room door and let herself in. I could only blink to find myself face-to-face with a girl about the same age as my oldest son. This tiny young thing—who was drop-dead gorgeous, by the way—was like a drill sergeant when it came to brassieres.

She took a critical look at my cleavage, reached up, and in a matter-of-fact way—using the only word I can think of—she fluffed up my boobs and then adjusted the straps. Which I will admit was a bit startling (and if I am honest, absolutely hilarious).

"Bend over," she ordered with a cheerful smile. Fighting back a laugh, I did. Then she reached in and hoisted up my cleavage even higher. "Now stand back up," she directed. Then she moved over to stand next to me and took a critical look at my chest in the mirror. "Wow, you're going to, like, *enslave* your husband in that bra."

I could only laugh. She told me with a cheerful smile that they had the same style in purple if I was interested. She let herself back out as quickly as she had popped in and left me struggling not to burst into shrieking gales of hysterical laughter.

The moral of this story is that a good bra can work wonders on your own confidence. And on a personal note: I am happy to report that the black lace bra did indeed live up to the salesgirl's prediction.

Take yourself to the lingerie department and get some sales help or drag a girlfriend along. Start working that cleavage. You will notice the difference in men's reactions. Plus, it's a delicious secret to know that you have on sexy undergarments. Maybe you'll let your man see that gorgeous cleavage in an extremely sexy bra . . . and maybe you won't. It is completely up to you.

charmed, I'm sure: attracting a new love

♥

Scent-sational Sorceress

> My soul travels on the smell of perfume
> like the souls of other men on music.
>
> *Charles Baudelaire*

What do you suppose you are telling men about yourself by your perfume? You may be surprised to know that the sense of smell can trigger many powerful memories. Smell and taste are from the more primitive sensory systems; they actually come from separate receptors in the brain, the limbic system. These senses haven't had to evolve in humans, and they are powerful and primal. From the earliest of times, we have been aware of the power of scent, and we know that they affect our psyches, our physical bodies, and our feelings. Perfumes act as a sort of personal signature. The scent draws attention to how you feel about yourself and hints at your intentions. This gives you the chance to attract a compatible energy.

When it comes to choosing your own perfume, the nose knows. You should choose a scent that is pleasing to you. Each perfume smells different on every woman. Try a few out, and see which ones you are drawn to. Or if you want to try a new scent, then take a look at these five major categories, and see which one matches up to your enchanting personality the best.

> *Floral:* Floral perfumes have strong overtones of true flowery fragrances. They may be a single note, like jasmine, rose, or lilac, or they can be a mixture of floral, which makes it a sort of floral bouquet. These are romantic, classic, and among the most popular of scents worldwide. These floral scents may be worn anytime,

by anyone, regardless of their age. Here are a few classic floral scents; see what your favorite single-note floral says about you: rose for sensuality and love . . . lilac for a first and true love . . . carnation for passionate energy . . . jasmine for romance and enchantment . . . lily of the valley for happiness and innocence . . . honeysuckle for a generous love and devotion.

Fruity: If you enjoy classic fragrances but want to punch it up a bit, try a fruity scent. These scents are invigorating and announce that the wearer has tons of energy, enthusiasm, and verve. Citrusy and fresh, they appeal to both the young and the young at heart. These types of scents can be worn year-round, as in the winter they make you think of tropical beaches and summer breezes, while in the summer they smell crisp and cool.

Woody: Earthy tones are the hallmark of a woody fragrance. Usually scents such as sandalwood, patchouli, and cedar are prominent in the perfume, and they give it an intense, intriguing aroma: think of a mysterious midnight forest or an enchanted woodland glade. This classification of perfumes is down-to-earth and naturally sensual for, you guessed it, natural, sexy, and down-to-earth women. To my amusement, I found that these fragrances were recommended for mature women only. Ha! I bet the researchers didn't talk to many Witches. This earthy-scented category tends to be very popular with Witches and Pagans of all ages.

Greens: The green sort of perfume is crisp and clean, like a springtime breeze or a clean meadow scent. They may have a hint of the forest in them, but think grassy plains and open meadows. There are two types to this green group, fresh and balsamic. These funky, modern scents can be worn at any time, and they are for the younger, carefree woman, a woman who is on the go, or a free spirit. Greens are a great match for the individual who refuses to be categorized.

Oriental: These are the perfumes with punch! Oriental perfumes are the strongest of perfumes with sexy overtones and rich undertones that often create a dramatic effect. These are the fragrances that haunt the memory and ensnare the senses. Oriental perfumes have a mixture of vanilla, musk, floral, and resins. They can even be a bit spicy or citrusy. They are best worn by confident, bold women who know what they like and are not afraid to go after their dreams.

These different suggestions and strategies that we discussed on enhancing a woman's intrinsic magick should give you many ideas on how to work your personal charm to your best advantage. This is fascination at its best. When you work with what assets you have, your hair, your figure, and your personal scent, you are working the most natural of magick. So work that charm—be mysterious, be confident, be fascinating—but most of all, be your enchanting little old self.

A Charm Bag for Attraction and Love
To Increase Your Magnetism

Charming people live up to the very edge of their charm
and behave as outrageously as the world lets them ...

Logan Pearsall Smith

Here is a practical spell designed to increase your magnetism and your level of personal power—in other words, to turn up the volume on your charm. This is a recipe for a charm bag. For those of you who do not know, a charm bag is similar to a sachet. It is a small cloth bag filled with aromatic herbs, flowers, crystals, and other magickal ingredients. Charm bags may be carried for any magickal purpose: health, safe travel, protection, to increase confidence and personal magnetism, and of course to attract love.

The directions that follow are pretty straightforward, and the supplies are easy to find. Just as any other act of magick, timing and supplies are important, so before you dive right in, take your time and familiarize yourself with the directions.

Happy casting!

Timing

A Friday night in a waxing or full moon phase. Fridays are sacred to the love goddesses Venus and Freya. Also be sure to work while the moon waxes in order to pull things toward you. Creating this charm bag on a full moon night gives it extra power.

Supplies

- A handful of fresh red rose petals and red carnation petals (the rose petals are for romance and love, and the carnation petals bring energy and a healthy passion)

- A pink or red sachet bag (you may use a square of fabric and tie up the ends with a satin ribbon in a coordinating color, or try a small organza favor bag)

- A small magnet (which will represent your personal magnetism)

- A small rose quartz tumbled crystal (this crystal brings love and affection; it is the ultimate "warm fuzzy" stone)

- A plain white tealight

- A saucer or small plate

- A drop of vanilla extract (for added attraction)

- Your favorite perfume

- A photo of yourself

- A safe, flat surface to set up on

- Matches or a lighter

Directions

Set this up in an area where the light of the moon will fall on your work surface. Place the photo of yourself on the middle of the workspace. Add a drop of vanilla extract to the tealight, and set the tealight in the middle of the saucer. Place the saucer holding the tealight directly on top of your photo (this will protect the photo). Crumble the petals from the flowers, and sprinkle a few in a loose circle around the saucer. Place the rest of the remaining petals, the rose quartz crystal, and the magnet inside of the sachet bag. Put a small spritz of your perfume on the fabric of the bag. Tie this closed, knotting it three times, and say:

> *By all the power of three times three,*
> *This charm bag brings luck in love to me.*

Set the sachet bag on the work area, making sure it falls under the light of the moon. Now light the candle, and repeat the following charm:

> *By the light of the waxing/full moon,*
> *Let my charm now begin to bloom.*
> *Fragrant petals do add their own powers,*
> *Lady, hear my request in this hour.*
> *My personal power is now magnetized*
> *As I close this spell under the moonlit sky.*

Allow the sachet to stay next to the candle until the candle burns out on its own. Once finished, tuck the sachet into your pocket or purse and carry it with you to increase your charm and magnetism. Dispose of the spent candle neatly, and put the

charmed, I'm sure: attracting a new love

saucer and your photo away. The remaining petals that were scattered around the candle you can return to nature and the Lady as an offering.

Now, as I am sure you have noticed, not only did the spoken verse work to increase your own personal charm, but you also created a charm (or amulet, if you prefer) to carry with you. Pretty clever, eh? Enjoy this spell, and be open to the magick that is all around you each and every day. Let your inner magickal light shine brightly, and allow the essence of love, enchantment, attraction, and charm to come into your life.

Next up: experience the magick of the four elements, and discover how to tap into their natural powers to bring love and romance into your life and the life of your man.

Chapter 4

Love Magick Is Elemental

What I love is at hand,

Always, in the earth and air.

Theodore Roethke

When it comes to loving enchantments, the natural elements of earth, air, fire, and water pack quite a punch of power. These four cornerstones of our natural world are filled with primal creative force, energy, and magick. In truth, you call on the elements whenever you work magick. They assist you in manifesting your dreams, your wishes, and your desires. In fact, having the capability to get in touch with and to make use of these elements is how we make our magick. To begin this process, all you have to do is open your eyes to the enchanting possibilities.

The four elements have a rich and varied history of symbolism, and they literally are all around you, in every environment, each day of your life. The trick is to identify them and to put their energy to use in your enchantments. Below, you will find information on each of the elements, with more details on how their unique energies are applied to magick. Carefully read these over, and remember that each element has a color, direction, and its own power to add to your magick.

Earth

Earth is the element of manifestation. It is a feminine, receptive force, and this element presides over the physical bodies that we live in and our solid connection to the natural world. The earth element is fertile, rich, and deep. Go outside, and dig your hands into the soil. Touch the textured bark of a tree, and draw in some stability and strength from the element of earth. This element represents that instinctive and earthy part of each of us that revels in our five physical senses, textures, and bodily sensations. As a matter of fact, the earth element blesses us with sensuality. The traditional color for the earth element is green, and it corresponds with the northern quarter. Natural symbols can be a dish of salt, stones, plants, and soil.

Earth is a stabilizing and steadying element. We draw strength from the earth, and it, in turn, provides us with sustenance. The element of earth is imperative to your enchantments, as this is the power that causes your magick to be born into your life as a physical reality.

Air

Air is, quite simply, the power of the intellect and of the mind. It is the element that exemplifies the power of thought, communication, imagination, and movement. Whenever you make a wish or get a brilliant idea, the element of air is responsible for the inspiration behind it. Air is a masculine type of energy and is traditionally represented as the scented smoke of incense or by the breath in your own body.

This element corresponds to the color yellow and the eastern quarter. It is often quietly symbolized by placing a simple feather on your altar. To tap into this element, step outside and feel the breeze rush over your skin. Feels magickal, doesn't it? Now take a moment and acknowledge the power of air, as it brings freshness and inspiration to you in many ways. The element of air embodies the realm of thought and intention, where all things live before they become actuality. Without air, our spells would not come into being.

Fire

Learn to recognize the power of fire in your life, from the sun that shines down from the sky to the natural light that illuminates your days. The fire element is symbolized by the color red and the southern quarter. Fire is a masculine, transformative sort of energy, as it is creative as well as destructive. The energy of fire is an important component of love magick. After all, we have the flames of passion and the burning of desire. The passionate energy of fire is the force that compels us all forward. In enchantments, fire is typically represented by candle flames. The dancing flame is a symbol of physical passion, magickal energy, and love.

In fact, fire is needed as an elemental fuel that is utilized to transform. As all spells seek to transform something, understanding the element of fire's power is a great starting point for many magickal practitioners. Yes, and in case you were wondering . . . that is exactly why we started out with candle spells in chapter 2.

Water

Water, our final natural element, is also a feminine power, and it's most often associated with love and emotions. Think about it: emotions can spill over or well up, just like the element of water itself. Water is a sensual and expressive element, and it is very easy to tap into this natural energy. Visit your local body of water, ocean, lake, river, or stream, or take a nice, refreshing soak in the bathtub. Water is a cleansing and essential element in our daily lives, for we are made up mostly of water; without it, we would perish.

In magick, water corresponds with the color blue and the western quarter, and it may be represented on the altar by a cup or dish of water, just as you'd expect. Natural representations for this element include the rain that falls from the sky, or seashells or a starfish arranged on your workspace. The element of water brings life to all of nature and is unfathomable, mysterious, and unpredictable. It is a paradox. The element of water is probably the most important one in love magick, because it represents loving emotions, feminine intuition, and deep, passionate feelings.

An Elemental Spell for Love

For this spell, you will need a picture of yourself, an envelope, and a representation of each of the elements. Options include a crystal point for earth, a feather for air, a small tealight candle for fire, and a seashell for water. Arrange these items in a circle on your workspace/love altar with the crystal point at the top, the feather to the right, the candle at the bottom of the circle, and the shell to the left, in between the candle and the crystal. Place your photo in the center of the circle. If you want to go all out, try sprinkling red flower petals or even little red heart-shaped confetti around the natural objects in a little ring. When you are ready, light the candle, and repeat the following spell verse three times:

> *By the powers of earth, air, fire, and water,*
> *I conjure up love, romance, and lots of laughter.*
> *May the elements four now bless all that I do,*
> *Help me recognize a love that is strong and true.*

Allow the candle to burn until it goes out on its own. Then tuck your photo and some of the petals or confetti that you used inside of an envelope. Keep this tucked in your purse or on your person for one week. This way, the elemental love energy from the spell stays attached to you, no matter where you travel.

love magick is elemental

Astrological Signs
Your Element and His Element

> We need not feel ashamed of flirting with the zodiac.
> The zodiac is well worth flirting with.
>
> *D. H. Lawrence*

The twelve sun signs of the zodiac are fascinating to apply to magick when you remember that each sign has an elemental association. Now, it is certainly true that there are books upon books about which sun sign is most complementary to which in a relationship. However, I wanted to tackle this topic from a more down-to-earth approach. When you break down the sun signs and put them into their elemental category, you make things more straightforward. And when it comes to astrology, I firmly believe that simple is better. Just in case you are wondering which element is assigned to your astrological sign, check out the handy list below.

Earth: Taurus, Virgo, Capricorn

Air: Gemini, Libra, Aquarius

Fire: Aries, Leo, Sagittarius

Water: Cancer, Scorpio, Pisces

This elemental-zodiac information can give you a good place to start when it comes to discovering which elemental energies you are most in sync with. Look these over and see what you learn about yourself. It will come in handy for future spells and enchantments.

Elemental Personalities for Women

Earth-sign women are sensual, warm, and affectionate. These ladies are real home-bodies, and they enjoy having a beautiful and welcoming home. Earth women, no matter what their budgets, will always find a way to create a sanctuary and a cozy haven, not to mention a garden. This way, they can indulge their passion for growing things yet still be practical while they are at it by growing herbs and a few veggies. They are excellent wives and mothers because they are generous, loving, and have a sense of fun, which they use in the day-to-day demands of raising their brood. Earth women are practical, down-to-earth nature lovers. Central to their lives are their partner, family, pets, and of course maintaining lovely gardens.

Air-sign women are intelligent, strong-willed, and decisive. These women are confident enough to stand on their own two feet. Air women are very cautious with their emotions and affections, which may make them seem aloof at times. They aren't really—they are just thinking things over and considering all the possibilities. This means if an air woman turns her attention on a prospective partner, she will come up with very interesting ways to keep him entertained and happy. Air women are likely to be the brilliant intellectual type, or they may play it more low-key and be clever and witty. Air women are quick thinkers, smart and savvy. They can express themselves well, whether that is through speaking or writing. If an air woman has a family, she will encourage her children to think for themselves and to be creative, outspoken, and independent. Bottom line: this elemental type of woman adores challenges and can be an ambitious career woman, strong, smart, and independent.

Fire-sign women are social, popular, energetic, and outgoing people. They are busy and active in their lives. Fire women are the multitaskers. Get out of their way, and leave them plenty of room so they can run around and get everything done—it makes them happy. These women make juggling career, love, and family look effortless. These are the ladies who manage to hold down a job, chair a committee or two, be a scout leader and a room mother, shuttle the kids to sports practice, keep their partner happy, and never wind down. They enjoy being busy and social. These ladies are warm and generous with their family and many friends, and they are also terrific businesswomen. These women are passionate lovers and terrific mothers. They can do it all.

Water-sign women are a mysterious and broody lot. They are as ever-changing and captivating as the sea. These ladies are quietly strong and prone to daydreams. They are intuitive, artistic, emotional, and have strong psychic talents (which they may choose to ignore, if they are stubborn). If this is the case, these ladies are "tuned in" in a way few can match. They always follow their intuitions but elect to keep this information quiet. This alone may cause them to seem a bit different. A water element woman may be difficult to understand, but she is a kind, loving, and sympathetic partner and mother. To this woman, both her feelings and her loved ones' emotions mean everything to her. She may be drawn to the healing arts and is a natural caregiver.

So, what do you think? Did you match up your birth element, or did you find that you were more closely aligned to a different elemental personality? If so, perhaps you are a mixture of the elemental qualities, and that is not unusual. The trick is to put this information to good use by understanding what your strengths are. Now, there are some of us who are dead on to their astrological signs and others who defy categorizations. For example, I am a Virgo, and I fit my astrological profile pretty closely and my elemental association of earth right down to the ground.

But just to keep things interesting, my husband is a Gemini, and he is the most un-Gemini-like person I have ever known. However, when it comes to those elemental personality aspects of his sign, which is air, they are much more compatible and fitting than his astrological sun sign ... which leads us right into the next section.

Elemental Personalities for Men

It's not the men in my life, it's the life in my men.

Mae West

Earth-sign men are kind, good-natured men who are content with the simple things in life: think of a skilled craftsmen who enjoys making things with his hands. These men are the big manly men, practical and down-to-earth, not the academic types. These guys are happy going camping, watching a football game, having a barbecue, and relaxing with a beer. They are inclined to be practical, hard-working, and financially secure. However, their definition of being "successful" may be radically different from someone else's. Earth men make great fathers, as they have a sense of fun and are willing to crawl around with the kids or help them build a fort in the backyard. Also, they may enjoy working in the yard and doing their own landscaping projects. They enjoy feeling the earth beneath their hands and want to have trees, shrubs, and (although they may not admit it) big flowers in the yard. Nothing too fussy, mind you, just strong, tough, and showy perennials. Earth men like the challenge of strong-willed women. Men of this element are generous, sensual, and very thorough lovers. They also enjoy good food and having a warm and inviting home, complete with rowdy kids and a big, goofy dog or a clever cat. They enjoy natural textures, earthy colors, and comfortable, sit-down-and-relax, kick-off-your-shoes types of casual environments.

Air-sign men are intelligent, oozing personal power. These men may be highly educated professional types or they may just be the sort of man who can be casually clever and ultra-capable. These elemental men hate restrictions of any kind and may be a bit of a "lone wolf" type. A good tip to remember when dealing with men who are aligned to this element is that these are the guys who like to be in control (or who at least prefer the illusion that they are the ones making all the decisions)! Air men may shift their frame of mind as often as the wind blows. One minute they are reserved and watchful, the next they are clever and outgoing. That sense of reserve may make him seem sort of aloof, but remember air men may be brooders. However, usually it is because they are so busy thinking about something else that is vitally important to them. Air men see things in black or white; for them, there are no gray areas. While this "all or nothing attitude" may seem frustrating, it also means that once they have made up their minds about something or someone, that's it. Air men are not going to be spouting off romantic declarations of love, but they are inventive and very attentive lovers. Once they turn their personal power and their undivided attention on to you ... well, look at it this way: you are never going to be bored.

Fire-sign men are always fashionably in style, confident, and optimistic. They are strong-willed but open-minded. These guys are enthusiastic, energetic, charming, and gregarious, and they run about a million miles an hour. With all that enthusiasm and affection, they make for loving husbands and very proud fathers: think Little League coach and savvy businessman all rolled into one. They are generous to people they care for, and are imaginative and innovative with projects at work and at home. Fire-element men are natural leaders and are typically the "life of the party" type. They have lots of friends, both men and women, and they enjoy spending time with them on various adventures of some sort or another. These men have an aura of excitement and adventure that is never quite restrained. Men aligned with the element of fire can be a bit obsessive and intense. They need a steady stream of love and support from their partners; this way they feel secure. As lovers, they are demanding, wild, and untamed. However, under all that ardor is a softer, secret romantic side. You just may have to let them know it's okay to slow down, relax, and show that tender side of their personalities, too.

Water-sign men are often described as sophisticated, intense, and cultured. They may be well educated, professional, a musician or a performer, or a passionate artist type. With all this water energy, you might expect them to be wildly romantic and every girl's secret dream. That's certainly possible; however, these men are often restrained and unfathomable, and may actually keep their personal feelings very concealed. While they may be very open and outgoing in public when it's time to take center stage and perform, they may actually have a hard time expressing emotions when in private, simply because those emotions can overwhelm them. You know that old saying "Still waters run deep"? Well, it really applies here. These men can be wonderfully creative and amazingly intuitive but prefer to play their personal feelings close to the vest. Others just assume they are clever and insightful, when what they truly are is extremely empathic and psychic. They may use these talents to their advantage, or, on the opposite end of the spectrum, water men can be easily influenced by a strong-willed partner. A water-element man is honest, open, and caring. He is supportive and generous to those he loves, and he knows the romantic value of a quietly held hand, a soothing touch, or a well-timed kiss. These men make devoted and adoring fathers and loving husbands. Water men are sensitive romantics at heart, but they are private souls and quiet about their very personal feelings.

Putting the Elements to Work in Relationships

Love at the lips was touch
As sweet as I could bear;
And once that seemed too much
I lived on air . . .

Robert Frost

So far in this chapter, we have focused on the elements of earth, air, fire, and water, and what these elements are and what they can represent when it comes to the magick of relationships and love. As we've seen, the elements also influence our personalities, and in and of themselves, they are a powerful source of enchantment. When you combine all this elemental knowledge wisely, you do indeed hold some powerful magick within your hands.

So, as we move on to the next few sections in this chapter, remember that fire energy is compelling, exciting, and passionate. Air energy is an ever-shifting power; it may be communicative, quick, and clever, or thoughtful, quiet, and reserved. The earth element is grounded, sensual, and practical. Lastly, the water element is intuitive and sensitive, with a deep, emotional energy. And now that you know what your element and his are, let's take a look at how they magickally work together.

> ***Earth-Earth:*** You two are both very down-to-earth folks, practical and sensible. However, that doesn't make you boring. You are both sensualists. This is an intense elemental combination. This pairing is probably the quickest one to get down to business. This is an unstoppable force of nature, so get out of the way.

After all, these two both love the same things: texture, touch, and being aware of the body's sensations and pleasures. You are both tactile, and the power of touch is never underestimated by either of you. Sexuality and strong, loving emotions are inevitably linked together—there is no separating the two aspects, as far as you are both concerned. While you are most comfortable in a relaxed and ordered routine of your lives, don't let yourself get mired down in the familiar. You would both benefit from camping or the occasional romantic picnic. Make sure you take the time to express what your feelings are—I know you tend to get caught up in the moment. But a little pillow talk or simple declaration of your love will go a long way.

Earth-Air: Here is an interesting combination. Air is comfortable with earth's dependability, while the earth person likes air's ever-changing moods. Somehow these two elements are attracted to each other. It's irresistible, and they can't help themselves. Earth signs can learn much from a talkative air sign. Earth signs are typically more quiet and thoughtful, and this can keep an air partner fascinated, because the other person always seems mysterious. Basically, the air sign enjoys the security and stability that an earth person brings to the relationship. Also, air personalities really enjoy the unabashed sexuality of their earthy partners. However, if the air personality is one who broods and is a quiet thinker, then the earth personality will have to remind them to come back to earth from time to time and to indulge in a little physical love and romance. On the other hand, if the air person is a talker, the earth person will have to come up with a pleasant way to shut them up. The direct approach is to usually hit the *off* switch of an air sign's thoughts. How do you do that? Try laying a big, sloppy kiss on them, complete with a full-frontal contact embrace. *That* ought to get their attention. They can only be cerebral for so long. Besides, this way the air person has something else to think about now … and it's something that is a lot more fun to focus on.

Earth-Water: This fabulous elemental combination is an extremely lush and fertile one. Romance between the two of you will have a more relaxed pace, slow and dreamy. Each of you is a mystery to the other, as earth enjoys the mysterious, ever-changing depths and movement of water, while water takes comfort in the sensuality and stability of earth's characteristics. Just keep in mind that water likes the game of slow seduction, while earth personalities want to get down to business and enjoy themselves, so compromise and learn what each other's preferences are. Don't forget that variety can be a breath of fresh air in your intense relationship. Go for a hike in the woods, make love outside, or go skinny-dipping. Read each other poetry or erotica. You are both sensual and revel in the power of touch, the act of love, and strong, deep emotions, so enjoy what you have found in each other.

Air-Air: Oh my, the pair of you need to work diligently to make sure that you are communicating well with each other. Putting a couple of air signs together can be an intense, enchanting relationship or one that is fraught with arguments and petty misunderstandings. You two simply have to communicate your emotions clearly to each other. Sure, you can both debate any topic night and day. But you need to talk *to* each other, not *at* each other. Otherwise, all that lofty air energy will create a distance. However, if each of you would completely focus and apply a bit of air's best qualities, such as ingenuity, insight, and attention, on the other, then I imagine you both will be blissfully happy in the relationship and never bored. The two of you excel at the art of seduction, so don't try to outdo each other. You could always step back and take turns being the dominant one. Should you need it, bring a touch of fire's passionate energy in your relationship and heat things up (I'm sure you two can figure out something clever).

Air-Water: An air sign can bring swiftness and clarity to a sensitive, laid-back water sign. Water signs may be overwhelmed by air signs that think so quickly and need to talk things out all the time. But water signs can use that soothing, calming energy to their advantage and allow a little of that calmness to seep into their air partner. Water signs can help air signs relax and feel. An air sign can remind a water person to try something different, encouraging new ideas and experiences. These signs are comfortable with each other's cool approach to love. Air personalities can relax in the embrace of a watery one. On the plus side, water signs aren't overly concerned about an air sign's shifting moods; after all, they have plenty of moods themselves and are happy to offer comfort. With this pairing, one of them is likely to creatively suggest putting all that mood and intensity to good use in the bedroom.

Fire-Fire: Whoa. Here is where things can burn quickly out of control. You two need to pay attention to your relationship so you don't burn each other out. That inexhaustible energy is a good thing, because combined, you two need it! The pair of you are so passionate and intense that you should remember to take time for just the two of you in your busy lives and activities. Use a little of that spontaneity and do something challenging and new *outside* of the bedroom that you can enjoy together. Remember to take time to express your feelings and the softer side of your emotions from time to time. I know you don't like to admit it, but deep down you both need to feel secure in the other's affections. Work as a team, not as the star and the sidekick. On the plus side, there will always be plenty of passion between you. The physical aspect of the relationship will be fun-filled, intense, and all-consuming.

Fire-Earth: Fire signs bring energy and intensity to the mellow and easy-going earth signs, even as an earth sign can easily ground a fire sign and keep them calmer. You will both benefit from each other's elemental qualities. Stability and practicality combined with energy and spontaneity make for an awesome combination. The earthy qualities of one partner allow the fiery qualities of the other a safe place to rest and to call home. The earth sign finds the passion and spontaneity of a fire sign irresistible when it comes to more earthly pleasures. Somehow, fire and earth become really talented at fueling each other's physical needs. As long as you are sympathetic to each other's wishes and respect each other's elemental strengths, you two make for an awesome pair.

Fire-Air: Since air fuels the flames of fire, this is an excellent pairing. Both of you are interesting and captivating individuals. You keep each other entertained, and you both communicate well. There is a harmony here, and you two make one refined and classy combination. This elemental amalgamation produces tons of energy. Air signs love that fire signs are fervent in their affections and can make those quick decisions, while fire signs admire the ingenuity and shrewdness of an air personality. Both of these personalities do enjoy their personal time and their space, and both of you respect that about each other. During all of the challenges and excitement of the relationship and the passion, don't forget that you'll need to share some quiet time where you can really talk. This way, you stay connected and can listen to and appreciate each other's hopes and dreams.

Fire-Water: They say that opposites attract, and this elemental combination can result in a fabulous relationship—or it can leave you steaming mad and frustrated. For the water-sign half of this duo, you'll have to keep in mind that your partner doesn't yearn for the nurturing, emotion-filled sensuality that you do. Fire signs are filled with energy, passion, and lots of action! You may have to tackle them to get their attention. If a water sign is sitting around and waiting for a fire sign to stop and notice that they are in the mood for emotional and sensitive lovemaking, forget it: you have to be more direct with them. You both have vastly different styles of loving and living. The good news is that fire signs find the water sign's deep emotions sweet and captivating, even as water signs find the intensity of fire utterly fascinating. So use that to your advantage, and go with the flow.

Water-Water: The pair of you share an emotional and psychic connection unlike any other. There is an ocean full of sensuality, and you are both empathic and intuitive enough to understand how to make each other blissfully happy and satisfied. However, you can also pick up and be affected by each other's moods and emotions. The ocean is constantly changing, and you can both become moody and down in the dumps from time to time—and, just as quickly, you can let the blues seep away and experience clear sailing. So use a bit of energy from the other elements and ground yourselves in the physical world. Talk to each other—don't just feel each other's emotions—and keep the lines of communication open.

A Sorceress's Seduction
Elemental Enchantment

When you arouse the need in me, my heart says yes indeed in me,
Proceed with what you're leading me to.
And it's such an ancient hitch, one that I would never switch,
Because there's no nicer witch than you.

Carolyn Leigh & Cy Coleman, "Witchcraft"

Now that you have an idea of how your elements complement each other, you can put this information to good use for an evening of loving enchantments. If you are trying to please him, take your relationship to the next level, turn up the romance for the evening, or simply seduce your partner, here are a few ideas geared toward his element and his preferences.

Oh, and before you even start complaining ... of course your preferences are important, too. But if you want to seduce him, then you need to focus on what makes your man the most inclined for romance and intimacy, because if he's happily in the mood, you are going to end up very pleased and satisfied yourself. Remember what we discussed back in chapter 1? It is *your* job to select and to attract a man. So, you have selected him. Now do the attraction part, and allow nature to take its course.

The following information is magickal. Just because you are not repeating a spell verse doesn't make what you are doing any less an act of magick. Consider that magick taps into the powers of the elements. When you focus on the main element in your man's personality and use that to make him happy, you are indeed creating enchantment. This type of seductive magick is not manipulative when you are focusing on pleasing him. In this instance, you are only setting the mood and leaving the outcome of the evening entirely up to him. Remember that a woman's power is compelling, fascinating, and magnetic: it pulls in what it most desires. These elemental, seductive suggestions should help you get the result that you are looking for. I wish you both an enchanted evening!

Enchanting Earth-Sign Men

For the earth-sign man, create a cozy, relaxed, and inviting atmosphere at home. Comfortable couches with textured "sink-into" pillows and natural items will make him feel at ease and put him in the correct mood. Play the evening low-key—earth men don't particularly care for surprises—and try a little nature-themed music to get the romantic mood going. Introduce him to your pets, and make him a delicious homemade meal of hearty comfort-type foods. Keep the mood casual, but try adding a vase of simple garden flowers you have arranged yourself on the table. He is sure to notice these over a formal arrangement from a florist. As earth men are tactile, try wearing fabrics that invite his touch, such as velvet, satin, or silk. Take a walk in the garden or a walk in the park. Hold hands, snuggle on the couch, and indulge in a back rub, a good cuddle, and some kisses, and then see where your evening ends up.

Charming Air-Sign Men

For the air-sign man, you are going to have to pay attention and see where his mood is for the evening. To help set the stage for the evening's activities, you could try burning some light incense or set out a dish of spicy potpourri, and be sure to wear your favorite perfume. Air men are often first attracted to a woman's scent. A little subtle background music certainly wouldn't hurt either; try something airy and Celtic, with lots of strings and flutes, playing softly in the background. Get things rolling by engaging in a little conversation, and make sure that you look directly in his eyes and listen carefully to his answers. Is he in a serious mood, where he would prefer intelligent discussion? Or is he more playful and light, where humor and laughter make him happy? Suggest taking in a movie, visiting a museum, or going to see a play. You can talk about books that you've read or hobbies that you enjoy. If you are home for the evening, keep the food light: try grapes, cheese, and crackers, and serve simple drinks or a nice white wine. Playfully offer to feed him a few grapes. Now that his attention is firmly on you, be direct. Focus on his mouth and lots of kissing. And remember—once you get his attention fully focused on you, just relax and let him do what he does best: be creative!

love magick is elemental

♥

93

Fascinating Fire-Sign Men

When it comes to the fire-sign men, you can pull out all the stops. Of course, candle-light or a fire burning in the fireplace will help set the mood for love, and it makes him comfortable. Play interesting or passionate music softly in the background. Have some fragrant red roses arranged in the bedroom to help set the mood. Break out sensual foods, such as a nice red wine, chocolate-covered strawberries, or a fondue. Try feeding each other in between kisses. Focus entirely on him, and keep your voice low and intimate. With these men, you don't have to be subtle. Physical contact is important, however, and you are going to have to be bold and make those caresses passionate ones. Whisper something provocative in his ear. Follow that up with a little nibble on his earlobe. If you like, you can try something fun and different—scatter rose petals across the sheets and wear a naughty little outfit or classic red lingerie—just surprise him. He'll love it!

Bewitching Water-Sign Men

The water-sign man is a different fish altogether. Showing that you care about his feelings and what makes him comfortable will mean a great deal to these men. As to the music, have several of your favorite varieties for him to decide from, and let him choose what to play. Serve his favorite foods and drinks. Keep the tempo of the evening slow and relaxed. A gentle lingering touch on the hand or a finger trailed down his arm will get his attention without overloading his personal space. Offer a neck and shoulder rub to help these emotional, expressive men unwind. You could suggest that you both go and relax in the hot tub, indulge in a moonlight swim, or take a walk in the rain (weather permitting). Now, while that might seem cheesy to some folks, he would probably enjoy it. Gently suggest it, and see what develops. Oh, and if none of those options are available … you could always soak in the bathtub together.

An Enchanted Evening

> Some enchanted evening,
> When you find your true love …
>
> Rodgers & Hammerstein, "Some Enchanted Evening"

I hope that you will consider trying out a few of these elemental suggestions. They should provide you with lots of ideas for conjuring up a romantic, enchanted evening or plotting an all-out loving seduction. Use this information as a starting point, and see where your imagination takes you and your man.

Keeping the Flames Burning

A woman who knows who she is is endlessly fascinating.

Marianne Williamson

Relationships have their own cycles and seasons. Keeping your established relationship or marriage vital is often a matter of attention—as in how much attention are you really paying to it? If things aren't going so smoothly, then either you or your partner needs to put some effort and personal energy back into the relationship. Keep the lines of communication open and recognize that a lasting relationship is always evolving and changing. It is a balance between romance, sexuality, partnership, and friendship. Your relationship needs care and attention if it's going to survive. If the affection and communication areas seem to be fine but the physical one is lacking, then it's time to work on that problem.

This chapter is going to be pretty honest. While I think we can discuss this topic without offending anyone, I do want to warn you that we are going to be discussing sex. Now, I'm not going to be too graphic. However, I believe that this topic deserves a practical approach, because let's face it: even the best of long-term relationships or marriages go through times when the love life gets a little stale. So, woman to woman, let's be honest, open, and talk about how to keep a loving physical relationship together.

If you want to keep enchanting your man, then you are going to have to keep him interested in the bedroom. Anyone who told you that sex isn't an important part of the relationship is lying (or probably isn't getting any). You don't believe me? Well, have you ever heard a man brag about how he *isn't* getting laid? I didn't think so. As far as men are concerned, sex is the coin of the realm, so to speak. Of course, emotional intimacy is important, too; so are love and a genuine fondness for and enjoyment in spending time with their lady. But, ladies, they are men. You have to look at this from their perspective if you want to keep their interest and have them stay enchanted with you.

Once the word was out on what new book I was writing, folks had plenty to say. Some of the comments were hilarious, some were silly, a few were insulting. Why people felt compelled to comment on this particular book during the writing process, I can only guess at. What was very interesting, though, was that the women's reactions and the men's were very different. While the men had many comments on this idea of "enchanting a man," 99 percent of the time the comments were along the lines of *well, phenomenal sex is a great place to start*!

On the other hand, the women rubbed their hands together and let loose a cackle. *Reeeeally?* They would practically purr as they pondered the possibilities. At this point, a slow smile would spread across their face and an eyebrow would raise. They would get this gleam in their eye as they'd ask, "How *do* you enchant a man?" Then they would ask what sort of topics I was going to cover in the book—and honestly, the sexual aspect of the relationship was about fifth on their list.

Isn't that interesting? Women were wondering about how to make themselves more attractive to a potential mate, how to become more empowered, how to find a good man, or how to strengthen their emotional connections with their men, in roughly that order. It wasn't until *after* the emotional concerns were settled that they started considering spicing up the physical side of the relationship. So what do you suppose this tells us?

As women, we need an emotional bond before we engage in intimacy, most of the time. We are proudly emotional creatures, and our feelings lead the way. While with men, they typically need a physical expression of love before they even consider the emotional importance of having a partner/wife who is also their lover and a friend.

Am I saying that men don't feel? No, of course not. I am saying that men react to love in their own way. Men can have their feelings hurt just as badly as women can. They are every bit as vulnerable as we are; they just cover it up a lot better (that is important to remember). Men are emotional on a completely different level than women. One is not superior to another; they are simply different. Obviously men do love, and they are capable of loving truly and deeply.

Sexuality is an awesome power. It is a force of nature, and as we've discussed previously, magick springs from nature and through your own desire to create change. Magick is love, and love is magick. So what do you suppose could happen when you

keeping the flames burning

♥

take that school of thought and apply it to keeping the flames burning in an established relationship? Why, you create a powerful and potent opportunity for magickal change. You will become a more confident and empowered woman. Plus, you will learn how to keep your man enchanted.

Bringing Passion Back to a Loving Relationship

Don't cook. Don't clean.
No man will ever make love to a woman
because she waxed the linoleum.
"My God, the floor's immaculate. Lie down, you hot bitch."

Joan Rivers

There is still an enchantress inside of you—but how to coax her back out? Well, if you've been reading and paying attention to this book so far, you should have a lot of ideas for enchanting your man. Also, all those flirting and fascinating techniques and the elemental personality information that was discussed in the previous chapters do apply to you, too! Just because you are married or in an established relationship does not mean that you give up your sexuality.

Tricks like slowly licking your lips, fascinating him with a bewitching personal scent, showing off the cleavage, and crossing the legs work, and they work well. Especially on a guy who hasn't seen those moves from his wife or partner in a while.

Maybe you should go back and read those flirting tips and personality profiles again. Now put on your witchy thinking cap and imagine how you could apply those tips to your husband or partner. Oh, and I'll just warn you right now—when you are already in an established relationship, those types of "Come and get me, big guy" flirting maneuvers will probably land you flat on your back, with your feet up in the air. Hurray!

Just how important is sex in a woman's life, anyway? It's vitally important. A woman's whole life is sexual. Intimacy may be created in myriad ways: a touch, a kiss, open and loving communication, and laughter. If your love life is going to be worthwhile, then you need to communicate. Let your man know what is pleasurable to you and what isn't. He is not a mind reader. If you don't speak up, how will he know what feels good to you or what you find particularly pleasurable?

Well, he won't. This isn't the time to be bashful. If you can't quite picture sitting down and discussing the topic casually, then tell him while you are making love. Don't start giving him orders, just whisper a few breathless suggestions. You could always nibble on his ear while you tell him what you like the best. Or take his hands and put them where you want them: simple and very effective. Communication enriches intimacy for both women and men.

Now, you can spice things up while still being yourself. If you are a bit shy and have a hard time imagining yourself going all out, then I suggest that you take this opportunity and learn something new. Or perhaps you are thinking, *I enjoy sex—I'm just not enjoying it right now*, or maybe it's along the lines of *Sex? Are you kidding? Who has the time or the energy?*

If you have small children, it can be tough to find the time for a sexual relationship, and children are exhausting. If they are small, send them to bed early and have an enchanted evening. Or get a baby sitter, and go to the movies. Sit in the back row of the theater and make out. If your budget allows it, rent a hotel room afterwards, or come home late enough that the kids are all in bed and asleep. Then, once the baby sitter is gone and the two of you are alone, go to your bedroom and let nature take its course.

On the other hand, if your kids are a bit older and can safely entertain themselves for a bit, find a DVD or a video that they can watch—something that will keep them entertained for a half-hour. Once they are settled with the movie, make a run for the bedroom, lock the door, and have at it. You never know, it might become a sort of code between the two of you.

Want to put an element of danger back into your love life? Try having uninterrupted sex in a house full of small children. Somebody is always knocking on the door, needing a drink, or wanting to know where Mom and Dad went. You may have to be quick like a bunny, but what the hell—danger and passion are a heady mix.

When my brood was young, we had a fail-safe Winnie the Pooh video. My husband would pull out that video, the kids would cheer, and he and I would exchange a significant look. That video lasted exactly twenty-nine minutes, so we would get the kids settled and run down the hall to the bedroom.

This is a very fond memory that still makes my husband and I chuckle, even though our kids are off on their own or attending college, and we have been married for over twenty-five years. To this day, Winnie the Pooh makes me sentimental—but for a very different reason than you might think.

chapter 5

♥

One Hot Mama

Motherhood is the world's second-oldest profession.

Erma Bombeck

The strangest thing happens when we find ourselves outnumbered and surrounded by young children. We tend to get into "mommy mode" and sometimes forget about the men in our lives. There are diapers to be changed, laundry to do, feedings to attend to, and then, Lady help you, potty training. When you are living life in the trenches with small children, you simply try to survive. It's enough to make the bravest of warriors cringe in fear.

There you are, wading through toys as you fight your way across the kitchen to discover that the toddler has pulled out all the Tupperware from the kitchen cabinet and is happily singing away while he tosses various bowls around. You neatly dodge an enemy missile (disguised as a Tupperware lid) with all the finesse of a hardened Marine fighting his way through the darkest of jungles.

Your sharpened senses cause you to whip your head around in time to see your four-year-old roller-skating down the hardwood floor hall. What is that he has on his head? Why, that clever boy is using a pink plastic bucket for a skating helmet. Obviously your child is a prodigy, coming up with new and ingenious ways to be safe while roller-skating in the house.

You make the mistake of turning your back to get out the baby's food, and your genius four-year-old is now skating in front of the baby, who is strapped in her highchair and waiting none-too-patiently for lunch. Oh, isn't that sweet? He is making her laugh while he shows his baby sister how to give you the raspberries. So from now on, every time you feed the baby, you'll get food in your face and hair. When the highlight of your day becomes *Sesame Street* so you have an hour of peace and quiet—well, as much as you can get with Big Bird and Elmo—you know you have a serious problem.

So did I make that last scene up? Nope, that really happened, and I have the photos to prove it. I can't wait until my oldest son gets engaged, and then I can pull out all those photos of him wearing a bucket on his head. I do have other incriminating photos of the rest of my brood as well . . . revenge is sweet.

However, somewhere in the middle of all the craziness of raising young children, your own needs and desires get pushed to the back burner. Your main goal in life is to carve out a few precious moments for yourself and, sadly, the hubby gets put even lower on that list of priorities. Sex seems like a distant, far-off dream. I should know; it happened to me, too. My husband and I had three children in a four-year period of time. The nurses at the obstetrics ward used to call me their frequent flyer. While my husband and I thoroughly enjoyed having our babies close together, now, when we look back at videos of the kids when they were small, we wonder how in the world we pulled it off, stayed sane, and stayed married.

Talk to other mothers of young children, and you will discover that while they talk about their children's accomplishments with pride, they typically have little to say about sex—unless it is to mourn that the love life isn't what it used to be. Becoming a mother does not mean that you stop being a sexual creature. It means that you have to learn how to divide up your time in more creative ways. Take some of the intensity that you focus on your children and turn it on to your physical needs and desires for the evening. Then consider how you can entice your partner/husband into your plans. Think about yourself and your physical relationship with your man for a while. Use your imagination; go ahead and rock his (and your) world.

Hey, moms are sexy, too! One of the three aspects of the Goddess is the Mother. The Mother Goddess is a fertile, creative, loving, nurturing, and sensual being. She embodies the very best qualities of being female. By taking a look at the finest qualities of the Mother Goddess, we should realize you can be both a mother and a sexual being. It can be done, and it can be done well.

Work hard at trying to keep the physical side of your relationship strong while you are raising your brood. This is vitally important. Don't obsess over every little thing, and learn to relax and to take some time for yourself once in a while. If you are happy, then everyone else in the family will be happier, too. If the Mother Goddess can do it, so can you. Make sure that you devote some time to taking care of yourself and to maintaining your own sexuality.

So, how do you pull that off, you may wonder? Well, here are a few tongue-in-cheek suggestions. Read these over and have a good chuckle. Then think about them and visualize how you can put these suggestion to creative use in your own life.

Love Life Lost Its Zing?
(What Are You Wearing to Bed?)

Now, just to show you my heart's in the right place,
I'll give you my best pair of pajamas.

Robert Riskin, It Happened One Night

I have heard many women complain that after having a couple of kids and being married for a decade or so, the physical side of the relationship just seems to lose its zing. Which makes me wonder, what exactly are they doing in bed? No, no, I am not interested in the particulars, positions, or graphic details of their sexual relationship. I am wondering if they go to bed only to sleep. Do they cuddle? And, for heaven's sake, what is the woman wearing?

It is a cold, hard fact that men are first attracted to what they see. They are visual creatures, and their stimuli are most affected by this. It's simply the way they are wired. So, if you are staggering into bed every night in old, ratty flannel pajamas, a faded T-shirt with holes in it, or a football jersey, chances are your man is not going to be inflamed with passion when he sees you. And if after having a couple of kids you fret over a figure that will never go back to pre-baby days, I suggest you start looking at yourself and the situation in a whole new way.

Have you considered breaking out the lingerie? Look for something that has a soft, satiny texture. You can find sexy nightwear that is comfortable to sleep in, no matter what size you wear. Trust me, you will notice a difference. It makes you feel more attractive, which puts you in a more likely mood, plus it looks (and feels) good to him.

A win-win situation. So maybe you dug out an old, reliable, guaranteed-to-drive-him-crazy little number from your lingerie drawer. Almost forgot about that little bit of lace and satin, didn't you? Or perhaps you went out and bought something new. Good for you!

Now, if you feel a bit nervous about trying this or are worried about how you'll look in the lingerie, then I've got just the thing. Let's call on a goddess guaranteed to help you overcome any nerves and boost your confidence and your sexuality.

Calling in Aphrodite for a Boost of Confidence

And now behold the Goddess seated on her throne …
receiving the adulation of her worshipper …

Sarah Fielding

Beauty is as beauty does. If you feel beautiful and believe that you are sexy in the lingerie, he will believe it, too. Beauty is an attitude—don't forget that—and confidence is sexy. When conjuring up a little extra confidence, we will call upon the goddess of sexual love, Aphrodite.

Calling in any goddess (the technical term is *invoking*) will strengthen the power of your woman's magick, or your spellcraft. There are dozens upon dozens of goddesses to choose from, so you will want to do your homework and call on the aspect of the goddess that best harmonizes with your intention. (See the appendix for a list of love goddesses and their specialties.)

For this particular ritual, we are calling on the Greek goddess of love and desire, Aphrodite. Did you know that Aphrodite is actually a Mother Goddess? You shouldn't be surprised. Aphrodite is a goddess who enjoys her pleasures and her men. This deity is adored by both women and men. You think the fact that she is a mother dims her sexuality at all? Absolutely not.

Now, when it comes to magick, Aphrodite corresponds to the element of water, as she rose newly born from the sea foam. Her colors are pink and aqua green, and her sacred stones are pearls and coral. Her flower is the rose, and myrtle is sacred to her as well.

When you call in Aphrodite, she sometimes takes you for a ride. She can be sweet and loving, gentle and giving, or she can be wild and wanton. Any or all of these personality qualities may manifest in you when you invoke her, so keep that in mind.

Aphrodite's Ritual

For this enchantment, you will need a pink candle (rose scented, if possible), a coordinating candle holder, your favorite perfume, and whatever style of lingerie that makes you feel outrageously sexy. You are going to need about an hour or two, so set this up when the two of you will have some alone time.

Also, please remember to use birth control and to follow safe-sex practices. (No, I'm not trying to scare you off; I am just being practical.) Common sense applies here. If you're having sex, there is always a chance that you could conceive. According to mythology, Aphrodite had many children—so unless you want the same, take some precautions.

To begin this ritual, take a luxurious bath. As you rise from the tub, call Aphrodite's name and ask her to lend you some confidence and help you feel more beautiful and seductive this evening.

Dry off, then slip on the lingerie. Anoint all your pulse points with the perfume. Go to the bedroom, turn back the bed, and light the pink candle. Once the flame is burning, envision yourself as a sensual, powerful goddess and a bewitching woman.

Repeat the following spell verse:

> *By scent and color, this spell is begun,*
> *For the good of all, bringing harm to none.*
> *I do claim my feminine power on this night,*
> *Women's magick, cast by satin and candlelight.*
> *Aphrodite, goddess of passion and love,*
> *Hear my call and answer gently from above.*

Now call your man into the bedroom and see how he responds to you in the Aphrodite-enhanced mood and the lingerie. You can figure out what to do next. Allow the candle to burn in a safe place until it goes out on its own.

Keeping the Home Fires Burning

Sexy and Practical Ideas for Real Women

> What this world needs more of is loving:
> sweaty, friendly, and unashamed.
>
> *Robert A. Heinlein*

Those passionate flames from the early days of the relationship are not gone forever, they are simply smoldering. They need a few good nudges to fire them back up to life. You can start this process by claiming some alone time for just the two of you. Then take a critical look at the other topics covered in this book and apply them to your life.

Loving seduction is a skill that never goes out of style. It takes a certain amount of confidence to seduce someone, so you have to be confident in yourself. You are an enchanting and bewitching woman. Turn off that inner monologue that criticizes every part of your anatomy. Here are some practical ideas to try.

- If you have had a couple of kids or are not blessed with a flat stomach, just lie down. When you lie down on your back, everything settles in and it makes your tummy look flatter. Okay, so you may have some stretch marks, and your belly isn't as firm as it used to be. Well, big deal. That belly held life! If I had to choose between my kids and a belly you could bounce a quarter off of, I'd take my kids. Women are soft, and they have curves. Be proud of the woman and mother you have become, and go with it.

- Find a short nightgown that hits you mid-thigh. (A little strategic camouflage, if you will.) This may make you feel better. Go for a short gown, something that has shoulder straps, so if your man wants to get at your breasts, he can. But you can still keep the midsection covered up during sex, if that makes you feel better. I doubt he'll even notice!

- Here is another idea, no matter what your age: turn off the lights and light a few candles. Candlelight is very flattering, and it is a woman's best friend. Need I remind you that a man invented the light bulb? If women had their way, there would be no fluorescent or incandescent lighting that harshly exposes every wrinkle, bump, flaw, or—heaven forbid—gray hair.

- Take the time to do a little personal grooming. No, no, I am not suggesting you go out and get a Brazilian bikini wax—by the gods, that's barbaric! I was thinking more along the lines of shaving your legs on a regular basis to keep those legs smooth. Porcupine legs are tough to lavish attention on, and we do want him to lavish his attention on you.

- Moisturize your skin, and pamper your whole body. Find a scented body lotion—or unscented, whatever floats your boat. Wear your favorite perfume to bed.

keeping the flames burning

- How about wearing your favorite sexy bra and panties to bed? Goodness knows you won't be sleeping in them. I'd be impressed if you managed not to have him rip them off of you in the first ten minutes anyway. And if he literally does ... I am sure he'll be more than happy to buy you something new that he can rip off of you again in the near future.

- Don't worry about your age. So what if you're thirty, forty, fifty, or whatever? Think about everything you have learned over the years about sex and love. That's years of experience that you can put to good use, and it only makes you more desirable, worldly, and experienced. I mean, let's be honest here. You think a real man wants to deal with a shy, trembling virgin every night? Hell, no. He wants an experienced, confident, lusty woman who can give as good as she gets in the sack.

If you first make yourself feel beautiful, self-assured, and seductive, your romantic interlude is much more likely to be a success. Be confident and take the time to prepare yourself for a little love. Now call upon your vast witchy wisdom, and go seduce your man. He'll never know what hit him.

The Sneak Attack

Love in the Afternoon

Spontaneity is the moment of personal freedom
when we are faced with reality,
and see it, explore it and act accordingly.

Viola Spolin

Sometimes, when you want to be romantic, you have to try the sneak attack. Oh, come on, you know what I'm talking about. Spontaneous passion is tough to come by these days for most couples. When you have to juggle your jobs, household duties, yard work, and the kids, I suppose that's why they call it "getting lucky." However, with a Witch's ingenuity and creativity, it is also entirely possible.

One witchy woman that I know was very clever. She was an early riser, while her husband was a night owl. Between their conflicting work schedules, she was often too tired at night for sex. During the morning, he was sleeping and she was awake. By midday, when she was in the mood, the hubby was usually at work. Their timing was simply off. As a result, they were more distant than either of them cared for.

One Sunday afternoon, their young daughters happened to be out with their grandparents, and she and her husband had the house all to themselves. Unfortunately, once their girls were off, her man zoned out watching a football game, and even though she had tried several times to get his attention and let him know that she was in the mood, he was only half paying attention. She considered whacking him upside the head with a skillet, but this seemed an unlikely prelude to an afternoon of passion.

So she quietly got up, turned back the bed, and lit a few red candles. She took a moment and called on a Sumerian goddess of passion and desire, Lilith. Lilith is a powerhouse of sexuality and not to be invoked lightly. However, this Witch had worked with this aspect of the Goddess before, so she was comfortable in her decision. Besides, she wanted to have a wild romp—a bodice-ripper type of lovemaking session, if you will—so Lilith was the natural choice. Confident in her selection, the Witch freshened up her makeup, sprayed on a little perfume, and went back in the living room to sit patiently next to her husband on the couch.

When the next commercial came on, she patted his arm and said something she had never said to her husband before. Perhaps Lilith influenced her, or maybe it was her own daring mood; who knows? In a casual and conversational tone, she told her husband, "You know, I always wanted to see if I could deep-throat you."

Her husband was so startled that he dropped the remote and just looked at her. She smiled slowly and suggested that since they actually had the house all to themselves, perhaps this would be the time to try. At this point, she kissed him on the cheek, got up, locked the front door, and tossed her husband a sultry look over her shoulder as she announced she'd be waiting for him in the bedroom.

According to my information, her husband did not see the end of his football game. Nor did he care. That afternoon he was a very happy man, who in turn spent the afternoon making sure that his witchy wife was a satisfied and well-pleasured woman.

There Is a Little Witch in Every Woman

Validation comes from within, not from without.

The God and Goddess exist within you.

Your inner voice says, "I am Sovereign. I am a person unto myself."

Laurie Cabot, The Witch in Every Woman

With all this talk about sex and enticing your man, I think it is important to close up this chapter by turning the attention back on to you. Here is an interesting thought: sex is not about what the other person thinks of you, it's actually what you think about yourself. Are you happy, confident, and filled with a belief in your own divinity?

This is the part where I tell you one more time that you are a goddess, so act like one. Men are more attracted to women who take charge of their own happiness. When you are an empowered woman, you are going to have a happier life and a much better sexual experience. As women, we should be both daring and knowledgeable while using our natural, incredible, Goddess-given sexual powers. Learn to create intimacy; this enriches sex for everyone involved. There is more to a sexual relationship than just the act of sex itself. A kiss, a shared laugh, a touch, mixing your personal energies, and sharing emotions are all intimate acts. All of these will put the love back in your lovemaking.

There are a few lessons we can learn from the Goddess when it comes to the physical act of love, the most important one being that if you do not honor your own sense of divinity, don't expect anyone else to. Enjoy the man or men in your life. Treat them as you wish to be treated yourself: with generosity, kindness, humor, a sense of fun, and love. Leave manipulation, power struggles, and mind games out of the bedroom.

Sexuality is a celebration, so be wise when you choose who you celebrate with. In other words, sharing your body with a man is the ultimate gift. If they do not see it as such, then they are not worth your time or effort. Treat your body as the holy place that it is. You are divine; you are a living embodiment of the Goddess. You are sovereign, and you are sacred. Sovereignty is a type of supreme power, and it is a position of wise authority. Remember that, and act accordingly.

Lastly, you, as a woman, are an embodiment of the Goddess. As such, you are a creative force. Sexuality is all about creativity: it is a sharing of personal energies, love, and trust. As an enchanting woman, you can create life or create new projects. You can and will create a deeper, truer relationship with your husband or partner, and you can craft positive and fabulous change in your life.

Believe in yourself, and the magick has already begun; as you will it, then so must it be.

Chapter 6

Bewitching Blossoms,
Bedazzling Gems & Beguiling Herbs:
Love Spells, Fascinations & Charms

I put a spell on you,

Because you're mine . . .

Jay Hawkins

hen you perform love magick in the spirit of "for the good of all," openly and honestly, you have a greater chance at a successful result. Love isn't selfish, nor does it seek to bend another to its will. So if you embrace the essence of love with a spirit of kindness and generosity, your spells will have a much better chance at succeeding. Each and every act of magick that you perform should be worked for the best possible outcome and for the good of all parties concerned. It is vitally important to remember that you should never attempt to manipulate another person's emotions with magick. If you try to, or if you somehow accomplish this, you will pay the price. Just don't say that I didn't warn you.

Just the mere mention of possibly manipulating another person with love magick will spark quite a debate between magickal practitioners. Why is that, you may wonder? Well, do you think it is fair or even correct to assume that you know what is best for another person? No, it isn't. So keep that in mind when you work these spells and charms.

You will notice that the magick in this chapter does not target anyone specifically. These spells actually focus on the spellcaster and their reactions to different situations. Most, if not all, of these charms and spells will close out with a "tag line." A tag line is a few closing lines that you "tag" onto the end of a spell. This ensures that the magick is nonmanipulative and working for the free will and the good of all.

Remember that a Witch's power comes from within, from the soul. It is an expression of their personality and their love and compassion for others. Magick is created through the natural powers of nature, your own wisdom, self-respect, and self-confidence. Keep these facts in mind, and you will find much happiness and success as you work your love magick.

It was fascination, I know

Seeing you alone with the moonlight above

Then I touched your hand and next moment I kissed you

Fascination turned to love

Dick Manning, "Fascination"

A flower fascination is a term I coined years ago. As discussed previously, a *fascination* is the art of directing another's consciousness or will toward you; to "fascinate" is to command or bewitch. Flower fascinations are simple spells and floral charms worked with fresh floral materials for any positive magickal purpose.

We will begin with our classic flower for love, the red rose. This blossom is sacred to the Greek goddess of love, Aphrodite, and her Roman counterpart, Venus. According to legend, all roses were originally white until the day Aphrodite walked among the wild roses and was accidentally scratched by the thorns. A few drops of her blood splashed on the white petals, and in apology the rose became red ever afterward. The goddess was so touched by the plant's request for forgiveness that she adopted the flower as her emblem from that time on.

As mentioned in the first chapter, roses, especially red ones, have been traditional symbols of love, sexuality, and romance for centuries. Their seductive scent is often captured in perfumes, and the fragrance of fresh roses crafts an erotic atmosphere.

During the Victorian era, the language of flowers was wildly popular. In this colorful tradition, each flower had a "secret" meaning. And it is this language of flowers that is incorporated into flower fascinations. A few examples: carnations bring enthusiasm and energy, daffodils symbolize chivalry, and tulips stand for fame and symbolize a perfect lover. Fragrant lilac blossoms signify a first love. Tiger lilies represent erotic love, while the daisy symbolizes innocence, and each color of rose has a different meaning.

By tapping into the language of flowers, you can work with the flowers' energy and magick. The spells in the following section are all based on the language of flowers, flower folklore, and traditional Witchcraft. You will also notice that all four of the natural elements are represented here in the various spells: elegant roses and lilies for the element of water, the practical and romantic tulip for the element of earth, spicy carnations to invoke the element of fire, and fragrant, old-fashioned lavender to call in the element of air.

Red Rose Petal Spell
To Call a True Love

> Red Rose, proud Rose, sad Rose of all my days!
> Come near me, while I sing the ancient ways . . .
>
> *William Butler Yeats*

If you are in an emotionally healthy place in your life and are ready to bring true love into your world, this is the spell to work. This spell employs fresh red rose petals. On an interesting note, when you incorporate rose petals into any spell or charm, it helps to speed up the magick, as the rose is aligned to the element of water and the planetary energies of Venus.

When it comes to procuring fresh rose petals, if you grow red roses in your garden, feel free to use those. Otherwise, a trip to the friendly neighborhood florist is in order. Ask the florist if they have any "blown open" roses. In other words, these roses are almost fully open, which means they probably won't be using them for arrangements—however, it will be easier to harvest the petals of these soft and open roses. They may even sell the blown roses to you at a discounted price. It certainly won't hurt to ask.

Directions and Timing

Cast this spell on a Friday, the day sacred to the love goddesses Freya, Venus, and Aphrodite. Work this spell only in a waxing moon phase, for as the moon swells every night during this phase, it increases your magick and helps draw new and better things to you. In this case, it brings a new love into your life. If a full moon happens to fall on a Friday, lucky you! Then the timing is doubly powerful for romance or love spells and charms.

Supplies

- A pink candle (for Friday and the goddesses of love)

- A coordinating candle holder

- Matches or a lighter

- Red rose petals from several roses (red roses symbolize true love and desire)

bewitching blossoms, bedazzling gems

- A small glass, ceramic, or crystal bowl (use a bowl made from natural materials, no plastic)

- A safe, flat surface to set up on, or use your love altar

To begin, harvest the rose petals and set them in a neat pile on your work surface. Place the bowl next to the pile of petals. Light the candle, and take a few moments to center yourself. Now choose a petal and name a quality that you'd like to find in your future love. After you name the trait, drop the petal in the bowl. Remember to keep this spell nonmanipulative, and do not call out the name of anyone here or you are crossing the line. Say things like "a good sense of humor," "honesty," "open-mindedness," or even "stamina in the bedroom." List the personality traits you are looking for in a man. After you have listed the characteristics of this man, scoop up the remaining petals and add those to the bowl as well. As you slowly sprinkle those remaining petals into the bowl, say:

May these petals help him speed his way to me,
And as I will it, then so shall it be.

Now hold up the petal-filled bowl to the light of the waxing moon, and repeat the spell verse. Say:

The rose is a magick and sacred flower.
Goddess, hear my plea in this midnight hour.
When I added these rose petals to the crystal bowl,
I've named the qualities I want my lover to hold.

Fragrant petals, full of power and might,

Send forth my request on this full moon night.

Set the petal-filled bowl back on the work surface/love altar. Allow the candle to burn until it goes out on its own. Just keep an eye on it, never leave a burning candle unattended.

The following morning, take the bowl full of petals outside. Turn to face the rising sun. Then reach in and scoop up the petals, and toss them as high as you can up into the air. Leave them where they fall as an offering to the love goddesses. Close up the spell with this line:

As the bright sun rises, this spell is done.

For the good of all, bringing harm to none.

Rose Leaf Spell

Choosing Between Two Lovers

Torn between two lovers, feeling like a fool,

Loving both of you is breaking all the rules . . .

Peter Yarrow & Philip Jarrell, "Torn Between Two Lovers"

If a maiden had more than one lover, it was believed, according to one mythology, that she should take rose leaves and write the names of her lovers upon them before casting them into the wind. The last leaf to reach the ground would bear the name of the lover

bewitching blossoms, bedazzling gems

whom she should marry. Old folklore like this always tickles my imagination. What follows is a fun, modern spin on old flower legends.

Directions

This spell could be worked at any time. I recommend that you do this spell during the daytime, so you have enough light to see which leaf hits the ground last. Take two perfect, fresh rose leaves, and gently write your lovers' names on the leaves, one name per leaf. (Write out their full names and use a soft-tipped pen or marker for this task. That way the leaf will not tear.)

Once you are ready, hold the two leaves in the palm of your hand, and hold your hand out and up. Now repeat the following spell verse:

> *Rose leaf, rose leaf, so supple and green*
> *Hear my plea, help me to decide between*
> *There are two who truly have a hold of my heart*
> *Reveal the best love for me with this Witch's art.*

Now toss up the two leaves as high as you can, and see which leaf hits the ground last. Whichever one does, according to folklore, is the correct man for you.

Of trembling winter, the fairest flowers o' the season
Are our carnations and streaked gillyvors.

Shakespeare, A Winter's Tale

The carnation is a flower filled with history and ties to many Greco-Roman deities. The carnation was sacred to Jove, also known as Jupiter in the Roman pantheon. The scent of this flower restores energy and imparts healing energies. If you've had a lover's spat and want to heal the damage done from a silly fight, the carnation is the flower to work with.

Listed below is the flower folklore assigned to specific colors of the lovely carnation. Keep in mind that a red and white carnation can also be used to symbolize the ending of a relationship. Conversely, according to other Victorian flower definitions, it is a way of telling someone that you are genuinely sorry. Use your intuition and decide for yourself which definition works the best for you.

White: True love and good luck (which explains why this is such a popular flower for weddings)

Yellow: Friendship and sunshine

Orange: Energy and vitality

Pink: Sweet, innocent love and affection; also symbolic of a mother's love

Purple: Passion and power

bewitching blossoms, bedazzling gems

Red: Admiration and love

Burgundy: Deep love and passion

Red and white striped: Regret; "I am sorry" or "I do not share your affection"

Carnations are a great flower to work magick with, as they pack a magickal wallop of energy, protection, and power. Best of all, they are inexpensive and easy to find. You can even grow a miniature variety of carnations in a sunny garden at home. These enchanting flowers are linked to the element of fire and to the sun.

A Spell to Heal a Lover's Spat

This is a simple spell; it falls under the category of "charming." First, purchase a few stems of carnations using the color guide and their meanings listed above. Be sure that the person who is receiving these flowers as an apology is open to the idea of magick. Then hold the wrapped bouquet in your hands, and repeat the following charm three times:

The carnation is a fragrant, spicy flower
Sending forth energy and magickal power.
By Jove, this flower sends healing energy true,
Now let's end the silly spat between me and you.

Now close the spell with these lines:

For the good of all, with harm to none,
This flower fascination is now done.

Finally, deliver the flowers yourself, with a sincere apology.

Please note: this carnation fascination makes an easily adaptable spell, too. This is a great spell to use when you have had an argument with a friend (male or female) or if you need to smooth things over with a cranky relative.

Tulips and Temptation

I generally avoid temptation unless I can't resist it.

Mae West

The traditional definition of the tulip, according to the language of flowers, is wealth, fame, and generosity. In fact, back in the floral vocabulary's heyday, the Victorian era, receiving red tulips was an ardent declaration of love. Tulips correspond to the element of earth and have the planetary association of Venus.

The tulip also declares an intense love and that the person receiving them is "the perfect lover." Tulips also symbolize the celebration of many happy years together. The different colors of the tulip each have a separate enchanting message. Peruse the following color magick list to see which shade of tulip best suits your goals or the theme of your love magick.

bewitching blossoms, bedazzling gems

Green: The wealth and richness of love

Pink: A sweet, dreamy love

Red: A passionate love

Red and white: Unity

Variegated: "You have beautiful eyes"

White: A lost love

Yellow: Sunshine, "I am hopelessly in love with you"

Yellow and orange: "I have passionate thoughts of you"

Yellow and red: Congratulations!

For this flower fascination, you may either use tulips that are growing in a pot, fresh-cut ones from your garden, or purchase tulips from the florist. Arrange the tulips in a prominent place in the bedroom or set them up on your altar. Remember to use the color of tulip that matches your intention.

Supplies

- Tulips in a pot or vase (your choice as to the color)
- A plain white tealight candle

- A candle holder

- A lighter or matches

- A safe, flat surface to set up on

Directions

Light the tealight candle and visualize the passion that you want to increase between you and your lover. Repeat the following verse three times:

> *Tulips are perfect to represent earthy pleasures,*
> *This fascination will bring passion beyond measure.*
> *This loving enchantment I do now tenderly weave.*
> *Petals and passion with the power of three times three.*
> *For the good of all, with harm to none,*
> *This flower fascination has begun.*

Allow the spell candle to burn in a safe place until it goes out on its own. Keep the tulips until they begin to fade, then dispose of them neatly. If possible, add them to your compost pile or to your yard waste.

Lavender and Violet Sachet for Love

Whoso loves, believes the impossible.

Elizabeth Barrett Browning

The fragrant herb lavender is associated with the planet Mercury and the element of air. Lavender is a traditional component in love spells and charms. A classic Witch's garden plant, lavender is a popular sunny perennial for the home garden. Its fragrance is old-fashioned, enchanting, and said to attract men. The violet is sacred to the goddess Aphrodite/Venus and is linked to the element of water. When you combine violet flowers' heart-shaped foliage and lavender together, you have a powerful recipe for a love and (rumor has it) lust-inducing sachet.

Timing

Create this spellbinding sachet under a waxing moon to increase loving vibrations and pull romance and love toward you. You can also work this spell on a Friday to increase the loving and passion-inducing vibrations.

Supplies

- One organza favor bag—try purple for passion or pink for love

- Fresh lavender flowers and foliage

- Wild violet blossoms and a few leaves (note: if violets are out of season, you may substitute an African violet blossom and leaf)

Directions

Stuff the little bag full of fresh lavender, violet flowers, and a few heart-shaped violet leaves from the yard or garden. Then tie the bag closed, knot it three times, and say the following verse while tying the knots:

Three knots for the Maiden, the Mother, and the Crone.
Empower this sachet and the plants that I have grown.

Hold the sachet in the palms of your hands. Visualize a bright pink energy emanating from the charm bag. Now say the spell verse:

Lavender for luck, lust, and for attraction true
Its charming fragrance enhances all that I do.
Violets are sacred to the goddess of love,
May she attend my call and answer from above.
Promote passion and love; may it help open his heart,
This sachet-spell is sealed by rhyme and a Witch's art.

You can keep the charm bag with you, on your person or in your pocket. You can also tuck this out of sight in the bedroom. Slip it in a nightstand drawer or tuck it under the mattress. And if you aren't feeling particularly subtle, then tie it to your bed's headboard.

This spell can be freshened up a few months down the road, if necessary. Simply dispose of the herbal components neatly in the yard, and add fresh herbal ingredients to the bag. Repeat the spell verse to kick-start the magick again.

Tiger Lilies and Lilith
Unleash the Tigress in You

> People who are sensible about love are incapable of it.
>
> *Douglas Yates*

Are things in the bedroom a little too bland for your taste? According to flower folk-lore, the tiger lily is a symbol of erotic love. And considering the color orange encourages energy and enthusiasm, this would be the perfect flower to put the "wild" back into your physical relationship. Lilies are associated with the moon and the element of water. For this flower fascination, we need to call upon Lilith, the Sumerian goddess of lust, love, and women's power.

Technically, when you invoke a deity you are asking them to lend their strengths and specialties to you. In a way, this is a form of divine possession. Therefore, it is not to be done lightly. It is important to know what personality attributes you may be taking on board when you invoke a deity into yourself.

Besides her associations with sexuality, Lilith is also associated with wisdom, equality, feminine power, and independence. Lilith encourages women to live on their own terms. She can be a powerful goddess to work with, so long as you remember that sex, like magick, should never be used to purposefully harm, coerce, or control another person in any way.

Lilith is an interesting deity. In her book *ABC of Witchcraft,* Doreen Valiente describes her as the enticing sorceress, the beautiful vampire, and the ultimate femme fatale.

Picture her draped in deep red and flowing black, with raven-colored wings and dark, flowing hair. Her eyes are the deepest black, and her skin is translucent and pale. She smiles slowly at you, and as her wine-colored lips curve, you might just get a glimpse of elongated teeth. Lilith is seductive, mysterious, gorgeous—and dangerous.

I have also found from personal experience that Lilith has a wicked sense of humor, so consider carefully what qualities you will be taking on when you call her. She will take you for a wild ride, so don't be surprised if you find that you feel a little hung over from the magick come morning. Of course, that is but a small price to pay for such an enchanted and wildly passionate night.

Supplies

- Fresh tiger lilies in a water-filled vase

- A handful of lily petals (to scatter on the bed)

- An orange candle for energy (your choice as to the style and size)

- A red candle for passion (your choice as to the style and size)

- A black candle for Lilith (your choice as to the style and size)

- Coordinating candle holders

- A lighter or matches

- A safe, flat work surface

Timing

Work this spell at night; this is Lilith's time. If you want to incorporate lunar energies into this spell, work when the moon is waning, or dark. Scatter a few lily petals on the bed, then set the vase of flowers on your workspace/altar and arrange the three candles side by side (be sure that the candle flames stay clear of the flowers). To begin, light the orange candle and announce:

To bring energy

Then light the red candle and say:

To inspire passion

Finally, light the black candle and say:

To call Lilith

Take a moment and prepare yourself. Now visualize that Lilith is coming to your aid and that she brings her gifts of passion and seduction to you. Now speak the verse:

There is a tigress inside waiting to come out,
I will be confident, of that there is no doubt.
Lilith, come to me, may I become more lusty and filled with fun,
Bringing erotic pleasure to the both of us, and harm to none.

Let the candles burn until they go out on their own, and enjoy your evening with your man. As soon as you wake up the following morning, close up the spell with these lines, which ensure that Lilith leaves you. This is a way of saying thank you and making sure that the invocation is completely finished.

> *As dawn breaks, I release you completely from my body, mind, and heart.*
> *I thank you, Lilith, for coming to me; hail and farewell, and now depart!*

If you are captivated by the language of flowers and these types of floral spells, please refer to my first book, *Garden Witchery,* for much more information, floral mythology, flower folklore, and fascinations.

Everything You Do Is Magick
Short, Sweet & Simple Love Spells

Every little thing she does is magic,
Everything she do just turns me on.
Even though my life before was tragic,
Now I know my love for her goes on …

Sting, "Everything She Does Is Magic"

Now, for those of you who want a "no muss, no fuss" type of magick, here you go. You will find lots of tips and ideas to draw love and romance into your life. These little spells and enchantments are short, sweet, and simple. They are for enchanting jewelry you already own, or perhaps they will inspire you to go out and create something new to bedeck yourself with. There are also easy herbal spells that take no time to do.

bewitching blossoms, bedazzling gems

♥

You can work these simple spells whenever the need arises. Or you can tap into lunar energies—a waxing moon pulls love toward you, a full moon lends your magick a big punch of power.

Also, don't forget the days of the week that are complementary to success, love, and desire. You can work on a Sunday for success, a Tuesday for more passion and energy, or on a Friday for love and romance. The little spells that are listed below require simple ingredients, just an item or two. The rhymes are sweet, and the time it takes to perform them is . . . well, short.

An Entrancing Garnet Charm

The garnet is a projective stone associated with the planet Mars and has the passionate elemental influence of fire. The garnet may strengthen the body and may be used to magickally tap into your extra resources of energy. Garnets will help you build up your personal energy shield (also called the aura) to its highest, brightest level. The garnet reinforces your personal power and announces that you are a force to be reckoned with.

Carry tumbled garnet stones in your pocket to draw confidence, romance, and love into your life. Wearing any jewelry that features garnets will do the same. It is whispered that if you wear garnet earrings, then you may attract a new lover. Charge the garnet stones, jewelry, or earrings with the following verse:

> *Garnets are a stone of deep, dark red that draws romance.*
> *Let your magick swirl around and a good man entrance!*

A Charm for Pearl Jewelry

The pearl has ties to many love goddesses, including Aphrodite, Freya, Isis, Lakshmi, and Venus. Pearls symbolize the moon and the ocean, so as you'd expect, pearls have links to moon magick and the elemental associations of water, too.

Now, some folks may not wish to work with the pearl if they object to the way the pearls are harvested. This decision is up to you. On the other hand, if you possess jewelry that has pearls in it, this is a good opportunity to work magick with an item you already own. Since the pearl is a lunar object, hold the pearl jewelry up to the light of the full moon to allow the moon's light to illuminate it. Then repeat the charm:

> *This jewel is charged for romance and love, bring it to me soon,*
> *Pulled in like the ocean's tide and bound by the light of the moon.*

Please note: before you panic, the second line in the spell ties the magick firmly to the jewelry, not to a person.

A Bewitching Bracelet

The rose quartz is a wonderful stone to work with when it comes to love and romance. This stone helps to draw love into your life. It also opens up the heart center, and its energies are soft, gentle, and warm. Here is a crafty idea for you to try. Let's make and then enchant a rose quartz bead bracelet to draw the sweetness of love and romance into your life.

Go to the local arts and crafts store, and take a look at the jewelry-making aisle. You should be able to find rose quartz beads, which are affordable and pretty to work with.

bewitching blossoms, bedazzling gems

String the beads onto stretchy jewelry cord, and as you string the beads on, one by one, repeat the following charm:

A rose quartz bead for romance and a rosy bead for love,
Aphrodite will hear my call and answer from above.

Once you have strung enough beads to fit around your wrist, tie the cords into a secure double knot, and then close up the jewelry spell by saying:

The beautiful rose quartz is a warm fuzzy stone,
This magick bracelet draws love but brings harm to none.

Herbal Love Magick

Keep rosemary by your garden gate.
Add pepper to your mashed potatoes.
Plant roses and lavender for luck.
Fall in love whenever you can.

Alice Hoffman, Practical Magic

Here are some quick and easy herbal love spells and charm bag formulas. The herbs featured in this section are easy to acquire and to use. Enjoy!

Ivy Leaf Charm Bag

According to old Witch lore, women who are looking to attract a potential husband into their life should carry a red charm bag stuffed full with green ivy. The ivy is a feminine plant, and it symbolizes wedded love, fidelity, constancy, friendship, and tenacity.

Remember not to visualize anyone specific here. If you do, you are crossing the line into unethical territory and working manipulative magick. So yes, you will once again notice a tag line near the end of this spell. Now it's up to you to decide what qualities you would most want in a husband. Try thinking along these lines: how about a guy who is open-minded, has a sense of humor, is a good provider, is faithful, loves kids (should you wish for any), and will love you unconditionally?

Or perhaps you are interested in a man who is cultured, sophisticated, driven to succeed, a deep thinker, and passionate? Well, decide what qualities are most compatible with your own, and then after you fill the charm bag with ivy, say the following verse to activate the charm bag's magick:

Ivy leaves, ivy leaves, you're so beautiful and green,
Send to me a worthy man, the husband of my dreams.
For the good of all, with harm to none,
This ivy leaf spell has now begun.

Carry the charm bag in your pocket or purse. Keep it with you for a full month. If you wish to incorporate some moon magick, start the charm at the new moon and carry it until the following new moon.

bewitching blossoms, bedazzling gems

Rosemary for a Romantic Boudoir

Perhaps your bedroom has become so overrun with clutter that it doesn't feel especially romantic to you anymore. Well let's fix that! The bedroom is a sanctuary. First step: get the television out of there—a mood killer if there ever was one. Instead, try a CD player, and select some mood music. Now, pick up and straighten the room, change the sheets, and put away the clothes that are stacked around. If you like, burn a few scented candles while you clean. Be ruthless, and pitch any junk that needs to go. While we are at it, haul out the vacuum cleaner, vacuum the rug, and dust the furniture. There, that's much better.

According to folklore, rosemary is called "elf leaf" and "dew of the sea." It is classified as a male energy plant. It is astrologically linked to the sun and has the hot elemental correspondence of fire. Rosemary has a long and colorful history of being included in love- and lust-inducing spells, so it is the ideal herb to put the romance back into your bedroom's atmosphere.

If you grow rosemary in the garden, go out and snip three nice stems of this piney-scented herb for our romantic spell. If you don't have a garden, no worries. Rosemary is usually sold fresh in the produce section at the grocery store, along with other culinary herbs.

To begin this spell, tie up the bundle of fresh rosemary with a red ribbon. Hang the herb bundle in the bedroom to induce a little healthy love and lust. As the rosemary slowly dries, its sweetness will scent the air and add a bit of herbal magick to your boudoir. Once the herbal bundle is in place, enchant it by saying:

Rosemary will induce lust and love, I believe,
Lend your power to mine with this spell that I weave.
With all the power of three times three,
As I will it, so mote it be.

Pink Rose and Peppermint Charm Bag

For our last down-to-earth spell, we will work with one of my favorite flowers, the pink rose. Historically, the pink rose draws love, and in the language of flowers, it symbolizes grace, beauty, and affection, which is just the ticket for this particular charm bag recipe. In magickal herbalism, peppermint leaves actually promote love, energy, and enthusiasm. This scent is bracing and clean. On an interesting note, this herb also helps to stimulate love. Well, there you go!

If you have a garden at home, these ingredients may already be available to you. If, however, they are out of season or you don't have a garden, then pop over to the local florist and pick up a few open pink roses. Tell the florist you are making a sachet, so you need "blown open" roses (you may get them at a reduced price). Mint is often found in the produce section at the supermarket, too, just like rosemary. If you can't find any mint, then improvise and use a mint tea bag. Just snip open the bag with a pair of scissors and put the tea leaves inside of the charm bag.

I would use a pink or white organza bag for this, or use a four-inch square of plain cotton fabric and bundle the edges closed with a pink-colored ribbon. Next, gently harvest the petals from the rose, and add a few to the charm bag. Layer the mint leaves and rose petals, one ingredient on top of the other, until you run out or the bag fills up.

Once the bag is full, tie it closed and activate it with the following charm. Set the bag on your love altar, hold your hands over the bag, and say:

Lovely pink roses and fresh peppermint smell so sweet,
Bringing affection and energy that can't be beat.
This enchanting charm bag of mine will draw love my way,
I'll be blessed with the grace of love for all of my days.

Keep the charm bag with you, in your pocket or purse. You may renew the spell and freshen the ingredients every other month, if you like.

Closing Thoughts

Where there is great love, there are always miracles!

Willa Cather

I hope you have fun working all these spells, fascinations, charms, and enchantments. Yes, I said fun. Witchy and enchanting women have fun all the time, because magick is a joyous thing. Remember to personalize the magick whenever possible. Try adding your own witchy flair into the incantations. If necessary, refer to chapter 2 and see if you can work these spells with the energies of the moon. Add a little lunar magick whenever possible; it does add to the punch and power of the spell. Also, don't forget to look over those daily correspondence charts for even more ideas and inspiration.

Always work your love spells for the good of all parties concerned. Keep a sense of humor handy, and tap into the wisdom of your own loving and compassionate nature, for these qualities will serve you well.

Next, we move on to yet another enchanting topic: the cycles and seasons of the magickal year and how to incorporate their natural energy into love spells and romance-inducing magick.

Seasons of Enchantment:
Fascinating Folklore and Love Magick for the Year

I loved you when love was Spring, and May,

Loved you when summer deepened into June,

And now when autumn yellows all the leaves …

V. Sackville-West

There is a natural rhythm of birth and growth, abundance and decline to the calendar year. Recognizing these tides and flowing with the magick of the seasons is very beneficial for those of us who practice magick. The holidays of the Witch's year revolve around the changing of the four seasons and the natural energies that they inspire. These holy days are called

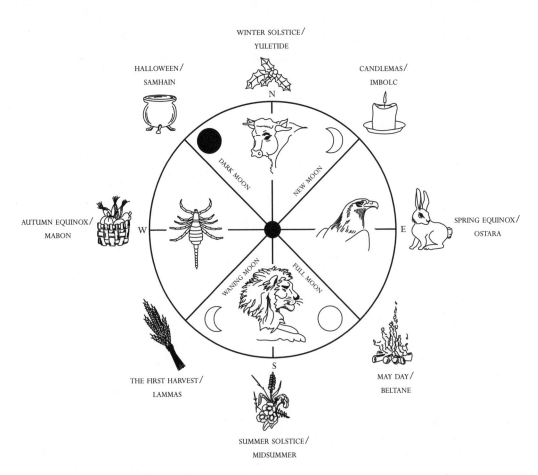

WINTER SOLSTICE/
YULETIDE

HALLOWEEN/
SAMHAIN

CANDLEMAS/
IMBOLC

DARK MOON

NEW MOON

N

AUTUMN EQUINOX/
MABON

W

E

SPRING EQUINOX/
OSTARA

WANING MOON

FULL MOON

S

THE FIRST HARVEST/
LAMMAS

MAY DAY/
BELTANE

SUMMER SOLSTICE/
MIDSUMMER

Recognizing the sabbats is a way of helping turn the wheel of the year.

chapter 7

♥

146

sabbats, and they each have their own stories, lore, unique mythologies, and magick that accompany them. In fact, when we work in harmony with the cycles of nature and the seasons of the earth, this gives us an opportunity for growth—not only on a magickal level, but a spiritual one as well.

The spells featured in this chapter all have natural associations and components that link to the specific time of their calendar year. For example, when you read the Lammas spell, which occurs early in the month of August, you will find that the spell works with the sunflower. Sunflowers are in season at this time, so it makes sense to me to work with the natural items that are available to us as the Witches' holidays are celebrated.

The magickal holidays follow a circular pattern, beginning at Samhain on October 31, which is the date of the old Celtic New Year. The sabbats occur approximately every six weeks or so throughout the year. There are eight sabbats in total, and as we work our way through the year, we are celebrating the cycles and seasons of the earth. Recognizing these days is a way of helping to turn the wheel of the year.

As half of the magickal holidays fall on the days of the solstices or equinoxes (the days that herald the beginning of a season), you will want to consult an almanac or an astrological/magickal calendar for the exact date. Why? Because the spring equinox, the summer solstice, the autumn equinox, and the winter solstice have dates that will change every year. For example, the first day of winter, the winter solstice, can fall on or between December 20–23. It all depends on when the sun enters the astrological sign of Capricorn.

If you do not have this type of astrological or magickal calendar, just look for the first day of spring, summer, fall, and winter on a standard calendar. These dates are typically the solstices and the equinoxes. Or just hop on the Internet and do a search for the solstice and equinox dates for the specific year.

Spend time in nature, and experience the mystery and enchantment of the seasons and cycles of the earth. Look around and see what supplies from nature are available to you in each season. This can add a whole new level to your love magick.

Halloween / Samhain
October 31

Friendly Fairy, Witch or Fay,
Fulfill the wish you wish today.

Victorian Halloween Postcard

There was a magickal time when Halloween was celebrated simply with a focus on the harvest theme, the mystery of the season, and magic and divination. Back in the day, spells and magick were considered charming. Folklore was all the rage, and a little mystery and magick seemed like just the ticket for the time of year. This period of time occurred from the 1870s to the early 1930s, with those last few decades in particular being a time that some Halloween fanatics consider the Golden Age. If you take a good look at the history of Halloween and how it has evolved here in the United States, you will discover a bewitching brew of folklore, fantasy, and fun.

The modern celebration of Halloween has evolved out of the Celtic Pagan celebration of Samhain (pronounced *sow-when*). Samhain marked the end of the old year and the birth of the new. This was the final of three harvest festivals, and foodstuffs were gathered in, the livestock rounded up, and everything was safely stored away for the quickly approaching winter months.

Many of the modern customs that became inextricably linked with Halloween were folkloric traditions brought to America by the Scottish, Irish, and English immigrants. The jack-o'-lantern, guising, fortune telling, love divination, and romantic love charms have all been absorbed into American culture.

Halloween Love Divination

On this night between the worlds, at the end of one year and the beginning of another, young women believed that they could divine the name or the appearance of their future husband. This was done on Halloween night using various methods, which included dowsing, using a pendulum, reading tea leaves, studying apple parings, or scrying into a mirror. Scrying, a magickal technique for predicting the future, is performed by gazing into a reflective surface—such as a crystal ball, a water-filled bowl, or a mirror. This type of fortune telling, or "dallying with the spirit world," provided a bit of excitement and added a thrill to the Halloween-evening festivities of olden days.

Directions for working the old scrying spells vary slightly. Typically, they are to be worked outdoors at midnight on Halloween, like the one here. Usually they challenge you to walk backwards while carrying a burning candle in one hand and a mirror in the other. If you'd like to give this old Victorian postcard spell a try, head outside on Halloween/Samhain at midnight with a lit candle and a hand-held mirror. Allow the moonlight to filter down on you for a few moments. Then carefully take a few steps backwards and then repeat the following charm. Once the charm is spoken, look in the mirror for a glimpse of your future love.

Round and round, O stars so fair!
You travel and search everywhere.
I ask, sweet stars, that you now show to me,
Who my future lover shall surely be.

Victorian Halloween postcards are treasure troves filled with divination, love spells, and little snippets of folk magic. There are very few old hags depicted; the Witches in the postcards are often portrayed as beautiful women, mysterious and glamorous. Perhaps that is why vintage Halloween art is so popular with modern Witches.

Samhain/Halloween is celebrated at a glorious time of the year. As nature puts on its final show of autumn beauty and color, enjoy the magickal atmosphere. Somehow, this seems a fitting tribute to the enchantment that Mother Nature has conjured up for us.

Winter Solstice / Yuletide
December 21

The holly and the ivy
Are plants that are well known
Of all the trees that grow in the woods
The holly bears the crown.

Traditional Yuletide carol

chapter 7

♥

The winter solstice is a joyous time of the year for many faiths. Also known as Yule, the winter solstice celebrates the rebirth of the sun and the return of the light to the land. This ancient festival marks the day of the shortest amount of daylight hours and the longest nighttime hours. Once the winter solstice has passed, the daylight hours will slowly begin to grow longer and the darkness will start to recede. The Yuletide festival comes to us from the old Norse Pagan traditions. These time-honored festivities include feasting, burning the Yule log, and decorating the home with evergreens.

The classic, natural decorations of fresh holly, ivy, and evergreen boughs all have Pagan origins. These plants have their own magickal qualities and should be enjoyed at this time of year. For example, the holly brings protection, the ivy grants a faithful love, and the evergreen encourages health and prosperity. As Yuletide approaches, why not combine these seasonal botanicals into a natural magick spell that encourages both love and light back into your life?

Yuletide Love & Light Spell

Supplies
- 3 large red candles (tall tapers or sturdy pillar candles are best)

- 3 candle holders, to protect the surface the candles are arranged on

- A few sprigs of evergreen to arrange around the base of your candles (the evergreen is a symbol of life and hope during the cold days of winter)

- A sprig of fresh holly (a male-energy plant for protection)

- A sprig of fresh ivy (a female-energy plant for love)

- A 12-inch length of gold ribbon (to symbolize the energy and warmth of the sun)

- Your love altar, fireplace mantle, or dining table

Directions

Line up the three red candles in a horizontal line across your work surface. Place the little sprigs or small pine boughs at the bases of the candles, making sure to keep the live plant material well away from the candle flames.

Then carefully take the sprigs of holly and ivy and tie them together in a small, attractive bundle. Tie the gold ribbon around the stems and finish it off with a simple bow. Hang up the bundle in a place of prominence, and enjoy it during the winter holidays. Now, light the large red candles, and repeat the spell verse three times:

Three red candles to symbolize the return of the light,
Now bring romance and illumination into my life.
Holly for the male and ivy for the woman.
Woven together and then bound with gold ribbons.
This solstice spell I cast to bring love and light into my life.
For the good of all, let it begin on this midwinter's night.

Allow the candles to burn for as long as you wish today. This spell is a bit different, as you can relight these holiday candles whenever you wish during the holiday season.

chapter 7

♥

After New Year's Day on January 1, I would then allow the candles to finally burn out completely. Close up the Yuletide spell with this line:

> *This loving Yuletide candle spell is now done,*
> *For the good of all and bringing harm to none.*

Clean up any candle leftovers. Dispose of the greenery neatly—add it to your compost pile or yard waste pickup, or burn it in the fireplace.

Candlemas / Imbolc
February 2

> If Winter comes, can Spring be far behind?
>
> *Percy Bysshe Shelley*

This sabbat marks the halfway point between winter and spring. Imbolc, also known as Candlemas, is a day often used to predict how much more winter we will have. If it is cloudy and cold, spring is supposed to come early. On the other hand, if it is sunny and fair, winter will hang on for six more weeks. In the States, this is also known as Groundhog Day. Even though this time of year may bring some of the harshest winter storms, the light is growing stronger. The sap is beginning to run in the trees, and a few brave crocuses are breaking the ground. Look around: you will see signs of nature beginning to throw off winter's embrace.

This is a perfect time of year to work a healing spell for yourself and begin letting go of old hurts and any leftover feelings from a past relationship. This day is sacred to the Celtic triple goddess of the hearth and the flame, Brigit. She is a goddess of healing, hope, light, and poetry. The colors often incorporated into this sabbat's celebrations are purple (for power) and white (for freshness and new beginnings). If you wish, you can add a few purple crocus blossoms from the garden to this spell. This would be very appropriate as the crocus symbolizes new love and, most of all, hope.

A Self-Healing Spell

Supplies

- Purple candle

- White candle

- 2 candle holders

- 9-inch lengths of white and purple satin ribbon

- A few crocus blossoms (optional)

- 3 ice cubes (if weather permits, use a cup of snow instead)

- A small glass bowl

- A lighter or matches

- Your love altar or a safe, flat work surface

Directions

Place the ice cubes/snow in a glass bowl. Set the bowl in the center of the workspace, and arrange one candle on either side of it. If you did gather a few crocus blossoms, then arrange those around the bowl. Place the two ribbons within easy reach.

To begin, light the candles and give yourself a few moments to center yourself, calm any emotions, and clear your mind. Now pick up the bowl, and say this line:

As this ice melts away, so does my heartache fade.

Gently set the bowl back down, and pick up the ribbons. You are going to hold them in your hands while you speak the spell verse. Visualize a bright, glowing, and healing light coming from your hands and into the ribbons. Repeat this verse three times:

Brigit, Celtic goddess of light, inspiration, and healing,
Help me cast away old hurts and embrace a new beginning.
This self-healing enchantment is begun on Imbolc day,
I'll move forward and start fresh, in the best possible way.

Place the enchanted ribbons back on the work surface. Allow the candles to burn out (please remember to keep an eye on them). Let the ice melt on its own. When it does, take it outside and toss it out your front door to symbolize that you are tossing away those old hurts and negative emotions. At this point, close up the healing spell with these lines:

For the good of all, with harm to none,
By my words and will, this spell is done.

Tidy up your workspace and dispose of any leftover candle wax. Tie the ribbons in a small bow, and tuck them into your pocket or purse. Or, if you prefer, tie them onto your clothes instead; that's up to you. Keep the ribbons with you as a reminder that your Imbolc magick is working to help heal you.

Valentine's Day Spell to Celebrate the Love in Your Life

While this is not one of the eight sabbats, it is certainly a traditional holiday for love and romance. We could hardly have a chapter on seasonal enchantments without including the big V day, could we? Valentine's Day is not about getting a fistful of diamonds or huge bouquets of overpriced flowers. No, indeed. This is a day to remember and to celebrate love. So on this day, I think a spell that celebrates all kinds of love will be just the thing, whether you are thankful for a romantic relationship or are celebrating the love of your family, kids, or best friends.

Some magickal associations for this day are images of Aphrodite or her son Eros, fresh flower petals, red hearts, and flickering candles. According to Greek mythology, Eros is the winged god of love who was often portrayed as a handsome, virile young man. He carried with him a bow and golden arrows, and those darts caused immediate love and passion whenever they landed. Whether the target was mortal or god, no one was immune. Eros is a god of physical love and relationships, and he was known to the Romans as Cupid.

The supplies and directions for the following spell are simple. However, this Valentine's Day spell is also easy to jazz up if you wish. You could sprinkle heart-shaped confetti or fresh, fragrant flower petals on the work surface, or add some fresh flowers in a vase. Use your imagination to personalize this spell. At this time of year, you may find heart-shaped novelty candles. If you do, try working with those. If not, no problem. Just use any style or size of red or pink candle. Choose red for a romantic love and pink for the love of family and friends.

Supplies

- A candle of your choosing (a heart-shaped novelty candle or a traditional pink or red spell candle)

- A candle holder

- A lighter or matches

- A photo of your loved one/ones

- Your love altar or a safe, flat work surface

Directions

Set the candle and the photos on your love altar. Add any other items that you choose to jazz this up a bit, and arrange them in a way you find pleasing. Oh—and yes, you may certainly work this spell for both your lover *and* your friends and family. Have one candle for your sweetie and another to represent those beloved family members and/or friends.

Take a few moments, and study the photos. Allow your love and affection for the people in your life to fill you right up. Then, when you are ready, light the candle and repeat the verse:

By the flickering light of these candles' flames,
I call Aphrodite and Eros by name.
Watch over my loved ones at all times, I pray,
I send them my love on this Valentine's day.
I thank you for the love that graces my life,
I celebrate my blessings this Valentine's night.

Allow the candle or candles to burn until they go out on their own. As usual, I remind you to keep your candles attended. Once the candle burns out, you may tidy up your workspace. If you like, leave the photos out for a day or two and enjoy them. Happy Valentine's Day!

Spring Equinox / Ostara
March 21

Spring, the sweet spring, is the year's pleasant king;
Then blooms each thing, then maids dance in a ring ...

Thomas Nashe

The spring equinox is the day when the hours of light and dark are perfectly balanced. Remember to check your calendars for the exact date and time of this astrological event, as the solstices and equinoxes do have dates that shift from year to year. The spring equinox technically begins when the sun enters the astrological sign of Aries, the ram. This spring sabbat is named after a Norse goddess of spring, Eostre. Some of the associations of this goddess are spring flowers, colored eggs (as they symbolize new life), and the hare, as it represents fertility. Why, hello, Easter bunny. Surprise! He's been Eostre's hare of fertility all along!

This is the perfect time of year to work a spell that signifies your readiness to start fresh. At Imbolc, you worked on healing yourself from any old hurts and emotional baggage; now, at the spring equinox, you embrace new beginnings and work magick to ready yourself for new love and relationships.

Fresh Start Spell

Supplies

- A pink seven-day jar candle (to represent self-love)

- Lighter or matches

- A rose quartz tumbled stone (to open your heart)

- A pinch of powdered cinnamon (for energy, passion, and happiness)

- A pinch of ginger (for confidence and success)

- A small pink organza favor bag, or a 4-inch square of pink fabric and pink ribbons (to tie up the charm bag/sachet)

- A clean cloth (to wipe your hands with)

- Your love altar or a safe, flat work surface

Directions

To begin, set the seven-day jar candle in the center of your altar setup. Gather your herbs, the tumbled stone, and the bag or fabric and ribbon so they are close at hand. Take a few moments, and breathe in some nice, deep breaths. Calm your thoughts, and center yourself. Assemble the charm bag/sachet. Put a pinch of cinnamon in the charm bag, add the little tumbled stone, and add the ginger. Tie the bag closed. Knot it three times; as you do, say this:

One knot for the Maiden, the Mother, and the Crone,
Empower this charm bag, both the herbs and the stone.

Now wipe your hands clean of the herbs. Light the seven-day candle and repeat the spell verse:

The past is behind me, the future lies before,
New relationships and love may come to my door.
A pink candle for love of self, cinnamon for happiness,
Rose quartz will open my heart, while ginger grants me confidence.
The stone and herbs now become a part of this sachet,
Let a new love spring forth, in the best possible way!

Keep the charm bag with you this spring. Allow the seven-day candle to burn in a safe place until it goes out on its own. It will take five to seven days if burned continuously. When I burn seven-day candles, I put them inside a large cast-iron cauldron. That way, if the candle should somehow get knocked over, the candle stays within a fireproof area. Other clever Witches I know place the burning candle in the bottom of their bathtub, inside an empty fireplace, or even in the middle of the kitchen sink. Be absolutely sure the candle is well away from any flammable materials. Safety first!

Here's a practical candle tip: seven-day jar candles are wonderful tools, but some folks cannot safely leave a candle burning while they are away from home. No worries—try this trick! If leaving the candle burning is not an option for you, then snuff the candle when you leave the house and relight it whenever you are home. You could say as you relight the candle:

Seven-day candle, burn, shed your magickal light.
As I am home and can watch over you tonight.

May the season of spring send new loving relationships, positive personal growth, and fresh beginnings to you!

May Day / Beltane
May 1

Tra-la! It's May!
The lusty month of May!
That darling month when ev'ryone throws
Self-control away.

Lerner & Loewe, Camelot

Beltane marks the halfway point between spring and summer. This is a night when the veil between our world and the world of the faeries is very thin. If you are feeling adventurous, you can always ask the faeries to lend you a bit of luck in love. Just make your request politely and leave them a token of your affection, and they will answer your request. According to magickal tradition, a small crystal point, a plain cake (cookie), or a perfect flower is an acceptable offering. Place the offering in a private spot in nature and leave it for the faeries to use as they see fit.

For a Beltane Day celebration, you can easily incorporate any red, white, or pink blooming flowers in the garden. The fragrant rose is a prime flower to incorporate into your Beltane magick. Try scattering rose petals in a ring around your work area. If you perform magick on a regular basis, then try sprinkling the petals around the boundary of your cast circles. The rose, as we have discovered, is traditionally used in enchantments to promote love. But here is a witchy tip: rose petals can be used to speed up your magickal workings, so incorporate them into charms and enchantments for extra magickal energy (basically they add *oomph*).

chapter 7

For your Beltane spells, try white roses to honor the Lady and her natural symbol, the ever-changing moon. Pink roses are for the fun and joy of being in a romantic relationship and will promote friendship and gentle affection. Red roses work a sultry Beltane-night spell to encourage love, romance, and attraction, and to increase passion.

Passionate Petals Spell

Perform the following Beltane spell outdoors. To begin this spell, sprinkle some fresh rose or flower petals all around you in a circle. You will need white, pink, and red petals. Repeat the verse, and save a handful of petals to close out the spell.

> *On this Beltane night, under the Lady's moon,*
> *I ask the Goddess to now grant me a boon.*
> *White flower petals for the Lady, and red petals for desire,*
> *Pink petals for joy and the fun they inspire.*
> *Now increase romance, send loving passion to me.*
> *I close this spell with the power of three times three.*

Once the charm is spoken, sit in the center of the flower petals and meditate for a while. Pay attention and see if you notice any faerie activity. When you are finished, stand up and bow to the moon. Take a deep breath and blow the remaining petals off your hands and out into the night. Offer a thanks in your own words to the Lady and the spirits of nature.

Summer Solstice / Midsummer

June 21

> Why, this is very midsummer madness.
>
> *Shakespeare, Twelfth Night*

Ah, the season of summer is upon us. The summer solstice, the first day of summer, occurs when the sun enters the zodiac sign of Cancer, the crab. Once again, the summer solstice will fall on different calendar days in June from year to year. So check when it is this year and get to work! The garden is in full swing now, so why not take advantage of the flowers and plants that are available to us? Work a little magick with the spirits of nature and with the tides of the moon as we celebrate the lush and fertile season of summer.

For Midsummer's eve, also known as the summer solstice, you could try your hand at faerie magick. Faeries love fragrant flowers, such as roses and blooming herbs. Oh, and don't forget those ferns in your shade garden! Ferns are sacred to the Fae. Adding a few fern fronds to your Midsummer bouquets is a sure way to honor the power of the faerie kingdom and to gain their favor.

Your garden roses, daisies, yarrow, and lavender should be blooming now, so try incorporating those blossoms together to weave a little flower fascination for luck in love and prosperity in the coming year.

A Faerie Bouquet for Romance

Gather together the suggested flowers, or take a look in the appendix for a list of other enchanting blossoms to incorporate. Use your imagination, see what you can conjure up. If you do not have a garden, then visit the local florist and pick up a few stems of daisies, a couple pieces of fern, and a rosebud. Be sure to incorporate a fresh rose bud into this faerie bouquet, as a rosebud represents the future, or what will be. Centering this in the bouquet will represent your desire for a romance in the future. (Please refer to the appendix for a list of rose colors and their magickal meanings.)

Now to the other recommended flowers: the daisy brings you happiness and is an expression of innocence. Lavender is protective and will keep misfortune away. Yarrow is the all-purpose Witch's herb and is also called the "seven-year herb," as one of yarrow's powers is that it is thought to have the ability to keep a couple happily together for seven years. Please note: if you do not have a garden, you can usually find dried yarrow and lavender at arts and crafts stores that will work nicely in your bouquet, and yarrow and lavender are versatile magickal herbs to have on hand for future enchantments.

Directions

Create a small flower bouquet, or nosegay, with the suggested Midsummer herbs and flowers. Finish the bouquet by adding a few fern fronds. Keep the bouquet diminutive, and tie it together with green floral tape or secure it with pretty red, pink, and white ribbons. When you have the nosegay arranged to your liking, take the faerie bouquet and go to a place in nature. Repeat the following charm:

At this time of Midsummer's eve, the Fae are all around,

On this ancient day, it's said, faerie magick shall be found.

This bouquet all wrapped in ferns I offer you as a token,

Grant my request for romance and love as this charm is spoken.

Be sure to leave that little bouquet outdoors for the faeries as a gift. Allow nature to reclaim it. I send you my best wishes for a most magickal summer!

The First Harvest/Lammas
August 1

To go by the asters

And breathe

The sweetness that hovers

In August about the tall milkweeds . . .

Denise Levertov

Lammas celebrates the first harvest and the halfway point of summer and autumn. This is a time of abundance and prosperity. The berries are being gathered in now and so, too, are the earliest of the grain crops. The summer herb garden is thriving, and during these warmest days of the year, things start to slow down just a bit.

On this magickal day of the year, try working with the cheerful sunflower. This practical cottage flower has the planetary aspects of the sun, just as you'd expect. In the language of flowers, it symbolizes success, fame, and riches. Sunflowers are easy to grow at home in the garden, and they are also very popular cut flowers these days. If you do not have any growing at home, check out the local florist. The stately sunflower demands your attention and always stands out in a crowd. Work with its magickal energies and you will stand out too this summer!

Sunflower Spell

For an uncomplicated spell that celebrates the first harvest and the generosity of love, try this sunflower spell. The supply list and directions for this love spell are simple.

Supplies

- 2 gold candles (representing the richness of love and triumph)

- 2 candle holders

- A lighter or matches

- Fresh sunflowers (in the language of flowers, success and fame), either in a vase or loose

- Your love altar or a safe, flat work surface

Directions

Arrange those tall, sturdy sunflower stems in a heavy vase or bucket. If you prefer, lay a few stems of sunflowers across the work area. Just make it as attractive as you can.

Work this spell as the bright August sun illuminates the sky. Light the golden candles, and turn to face the sun. Close your eyes and tip up your face to the warm sunlight that is streaming down on you. Announce out loud, in your own words, your goals for an abundant, successful life and a fulfilling love. Then repeat the verse three times:

On this Lammas day, the sun shines so warm and bright,
I'll work magick to bring my hopes and dreams to light.
Like a golden sunflower, I turn to face the sun,
Bring me success, abundance, and love so true and fun.
This sunflower sabbat love spell is now gently spun,
With my words, magick flows, and change is truly begun.

Allow the candles to burn in a safe place until they go out on their own. Let the sunflowers dry out. Harvest the petals for use in other spells and charms that call for success and abundance. Place the dried seed heads outside so the birds can eat the seed as a snack.

Autumn Equinox / Mabon
September 21

There is a harmony

In autumn, and a luster in its sky ...

Percy Bysshe Shelley

At the autumnal equinox, we once again have a day with equal hours of both day and night. Like the spring equinox, this autumn holiday is a time of balance, too. The autumn equinox commences as the sun rolls into the astrological sign of Libra, whose scales are a fitting symbol for this colorful point of the year. This holiday is a celebration of gathering in and reaping the last of the fruit and grain crops. It is often called the Witches' Thanksgiving, and it is indeed a time to be appreciative of the blessings in your life, for we are rejoicing in the harvest and the bounty of the earth.

The apple plays a large part in this September festival. After all, apples are in season. The apple is a natural symbol of wisdom and love magick; it was associated with many gods and goddesses of love. And, as I am sure many of you know, if you slice an apple crosswise you will discover the star of knowledge inside.

Apples were often incorporated into love divination. If you wished to discover the name of your true love, then you had to pare an apple in an unbroken chain. Once the apple is pared, flip the apple peel over your shoulder, into a previously placed pot of water. The peel will unfurl in the water, taking the shape of the first letter of the first name of your true love.

Apple Lore for Love

According to old wise woman lore, the number of apple seeds found inside the apple may tell your fortune in love. This requires you to eat the apple and then carefully cut up the apple core to count the seeds. Once you have them accounted for, here is the old apple seed rhyme. Check it out and see how you did!

One, I love; two, I love;
Three, I love, I say;
Four, I love with all my heart;
Five, I cast away.
Six, he loves; seven, she loves;
Eight, they both agree;
Nine, he comes; ten, he tarries;
Eleven, he courts; twelve, he marries.

As the wheel of the year turns, the seasons slowly change as we celebrate the magickal holidays. No matter what time of year it is, there is always a reason to rejoice and be happy. There is much to be learned by following and celebrating the changing cycles and seasons of the magickal year. These holidays have many levels, both culturally and spiritually, to explore. Pay attention to the natural rhythms of the year, and you will find that your magick is easier to access and to perform—for when you work in harmony with the cycles of nature, positive, loving change is entirely possible.

The Dark Side of Love

If this be love, to clothe me with dark thoughts,
Haunting untrodden paths to wail apart;
My pleasures horror, music tragic notes,
Tears in mine eyes and sorrow at my heart...

Samuel Daniel

I will confess that when I started this book, I thought it would be a lot of fun to write, and it certainly has been. But somewhere along the way, I stopped thinking only along the lines of a romp in the satin sheets, candlelight, and fun magick, with a good measure of girl power thrown in.

I knew there would be much more depth to the topic when I started writing about Craft ethics right off the bat in the first chapter. The Goddess was guiding my hand even then, I believe. For myself, female empowerment became an even more important concept to emphasize as the book began to come to life. Yes, the chapters on flirtation and seduction were fun. They were supposed to be! So I smiled, laughed, and kept on writing. Then something interesting happened.

As I began to wade deeper into the topic, I realized there was a lot of ground to cover here. Magick and the empowerment of women can and does happen every day and at any time during the year. However, some of the topics concerning love magick are darker and heavier than others.

So with this in mind, I believe that it is time to discuss the darker side of love and emotions. As enchanting women, we know that with the light comes the dark, and that the dark is not to be feared. It is simply part of the duality of nature and of the human experience. Honestly, love isn't all confetti hearts tossed in the air, dancing in the rain, and weeping violin serenades. Sometimes it's stressful, raw, and hurtful. Whenever we let go of a failing relationship, when one comes to an abrupt end, or when we deal with our darker emotions, it is a painful process.

This is not always a negative thing. Growth requires change. Not all change is smooth; it can be chaotic and messy. What is important to keep in mind is that bringing something new into the world requires the inevitable labor and birthing pains.

Witches and other magick users tend to be very sensitive, or empathic, if you prefer that term. This sensitivity and susceptibility to emotions in general, and to other people's emotional states of mind and their feelings, can become a double-edged sword if Witches are not careful.

So, consider that your thoughts and emotions are the real generators of magickal energy, for they basically fuel your spellwork. Negative emotions, hatred, and jealousy will need to be firmly set aside, as they have no place while you work any kind of magick. You do have a right to express your feelings, and sometimes a good cry or rant will help you feel better as nothing else can. However, you will want to get that out of your system before you start working the magick in this chapter (or any other, for that matter).

Put your game face on and be settled, calm, and centered before you start casting. Think about how your magickal actions will affect your world. Working magick when you are emotionally distraught is never a good idea. Magick creates change. It also follows the path of least resistance. So be absolutely sure you will send out positive change for yourself and anyone else. Realistically, that positive change may be along the lines of "I wish you well, and I wish you far, far away."

Something that I stress in all of my books is that true magick comes from the heart. Keep your common sense handy, and consider the bigger picture. Always remember that when you work compassionate magick from the heart, while keeping your own darker emotions, such as anger or jealousy, under control, you have a winning combination.

Charms, Fascinations, Spells & Rituals
The Subtle Differences

> Spells are a means of positioning and negotiating,
>
> the same friendly persuasion found in the gentle art of seduction,
>
> but on the psychic level.

Laurie Cabot, Love Magic

In this chapter, the magick is more involved and lengthier. Some of these spells cross over to become more involved rituals. So what is the difference between a charm, enchantment, fascination, spell, and ritual, you may ask? The answer would be the length of time it takes you to perform it, the amount of components required, and finally the level of knowledge that it takes to work the particular act of magick.

A simple charm is a visualization or a quickly spoken verse, perhaps with an item or two, such as a crystal or herb, to empower, much like the charm bag directions found in the earlier chapters. A fascination takes personal power, focus, and, in the case of a flower fascination, the addition of one key magickal flower.

An enchantment or a spell (this term is sometimes used interchangeably) will take a bit longer, requiring more focus and more personal power. The use of astrological timing will be incorporated, such as the phase of the moon and/or the day of the week. Also, the spell or enchantment will probably include lighting a candle, working with the four natural elements, or requesting the assistance of a deity. Visualization techniques may also be employed. The spell or enchantment has definite steps, procedures, and various supplies—crystals, herbs, and specific colored or scented candles are typically used.

chapter 8

♥

Lastly, a ritual has all of the listed components from above, and it typically has many steps and several supplies. It is more formal and may take hours or even days to perform. Now, before you start hopping up and down, all ready to tell me that sometimes spells, charms, fascinations, and rituals all share similar components and techniques . . . I will agree with you.

Yes, you are absolutely correct. The bottom line here, girls, is this: the quantity of the components required, the amount of personal energy spent, the actual length of time it takes you to perform the task, and finally the level of seriousness required will define the difference. There is a reason that these more serious rituals and spells are in the back of the book.

If you have been paying attention, you have noticed that we started out with simple techniques and lighter topics to warm you up. As we worked our way to the middle sections of the book, you had the chance to flex your magickal muscles and to lovingly grow, laugh, and learn. Ah, you see? There is a method to my madness.

Remember to check in with your intuition and listen to your own inner voice when you work your charms, spells, and rituals. The magick in this book will bring real change to your life, and that transformation may surprise you. Pay attention to that personal moral compass, and follow your own ethics. This will serve you very well. These compassionate qualities will clue you in on how best to proceed. So stop, center, listen, and carefully reflect on all your options. Consider everything that you have learned about the Craft so far.

Now, let's get to work!

A Spell to Protect Your Man

You say you're gonna take him
But I don't believe you can
'Cause you ain't woman enough to take my man...

Loretta Lynn, "You Ain't Woman Enough"

Ah, the stories I could tell you...This is a very popular topic, and I often get asked the wildest questions from teary-eyed, frantic women who do not practice magick but pounce on me because I am a Witch. They are absolutely convinced that some tramp has put an evil spell on their man. The story goes that the husband couldn't help himself from cheating on his wife. It was all an "evil love spell"—not his fault at all. He was just a mindless type of love-slave—a veritable zombie—a victim, if you will. Why, those poor little lambs! (Yes, that was sarcasm.)

In reality, that type of spell is very, very rare. Is it possible? I suppose it might be, but the cost to the caster would be incredible, for they would not be able to maintain that depth of emotional manipulation for any length of time. In all probability, this is just a rather inventive excuse that the husband came up with when he got caught cheating. Sad, but true. So don't fall for it.

The next spell is for those times when you know another woman is sniffing around your man, which is tough because typically your guy doesn't have a clue. (Classically, men don't pay attention to things like this. It usually takes some over-the-top moves before they figure it out.)

Unfortunately, the more aggressive you act toward the other woman, even if this behavior is deserved, the more you'll look like a bitch to your husband/partner. Or if you get overprotective of your man, then you may appear to be insecure and jealous—especially if he isn't clueing in to the potential problem.

What follows is not a spell designed to fix your insecurities. This a spell to protect a good man and your loving relationship. This type of kitchen magick employs the power of ice and is sometimes referred to as "freezer magick." It helps volatile situations cool off so everyone will calm down (especially you). This will also help buy you some time and make the troublemaker feel a bit guilty about their actions and cool off their pursuit.

The Ice, Thorn & Herb Spell

Supplies

- A slip of paper with the troublemaker's first and last name on it (if you can get their signature, that's even better)

- A dark red rose with leaves and the thorns on the stem

- A pair of kitchen scissors

- A small disposable food container with a lid (for the freezer)

- A pinch of salt (to remove any negativity)

- A pinch of garlic powder (to neutralize nasty gossip)

- A cup or two of water

- Your freezer

Directions

Work this spell at any time. To begin, cut the rosebud neatly off of the stem. Set the flower aside. Next, gently wrap the name of the troublemaker around the rose stem. Let a thorn pierce the paper. Now take the thorny, leafy stem and carefully bend it in half so it will fit inside the container. Add enough water to cover. Then sprinkle in a pinch of salt to remove any negativity and a pinch of garlic powder to neutralize gossip. Seal the container, and set it on your work area. Repeat the spell verse three times:

> *Chill out! Your affections will now turn cold,*
> *For this is my man that I have and hold.*
> *Rose thorns to prick your conscious and to make you leave,*
> *You'll cause no more strife between my lover and me.*
> *Sealed up tight with herbs and a rhyme,*
> *This freezer magick turns out fine!*

Put the container in the freezer and smartly close the door. Say these lines to close up the spell:

> *For the good of all and with harm to none,*
> *By ice, thorn, and herbs, this spell is now done.*

Let it freeze solid. Leave it in the freezer until the situation works itself out. Don't fret about the situation anymore. Finally, take the rose bud that you set aside, strip the petals, and scatter them across the bed sheets. Go find your man, and invite him to the bedroom for a physical celebration of your love.

Men—
Can't Live with 'em, Can't Turn 'em Into Newts

I love being married.
It's so great to find that one special person
you want to annoy for the rest of your life.

Rita Rudner

Every relationship goes through tough times. Perhaps it's financial difficulties, an illness, bickering over daily tasks, trouble with the kids, or the in-laws. Maybe the two of you are standing on opposite sides of an issue, you are both angry, and nothing is being resolved. So, what are your options? Well, common sense tells us that you two need to talk it out. That's *talk*, not shout. Try to reach a compromise or agree to disagree. Focus on what you love about each other. Of course, there will always be little things about your man that will drive you crazy, and vice versa. After twenty-five years of marriage, I am not going to tell you that my married life has been a fairy tale. Hell, no. We have our good days and our bad days, just like any other couple.

For example, I can't take my husband to a home improvement store. The minute I turn my back on him, he disappears. It's like magick. *Poof!* And he's gone! So, unless I want to hold his hand the entire time to keep him next to me (not unlike a toddler), I can plan on spending at least fifteen minutes each visit tracking my guy down. Eventually, when I find him, it makes me crazy to have him look at me and ask, "Where did you go?"

By the time I find him—and what in the world was he doing looking at front doors, anyway? Yes, I see the leaded-glass panels, and I don't care. We came in to look at new bathroom lights, didn't we?—I am one aggravated and pissy woman.

I mean, jeez! Is it so hard to tell your wife if you decide to wander off and go look at something else? Only a man could lose a freaking half-hour looking at lumber. I mean, come on. Get a flat board of plywood or a straight two-by-four, and let's *go,* already! I actually have a goal of being able to visit a home improvement store and walk out of it without getting into a tiff with my guy. It's become my nirvana.

These kinds of petty aggravations and silly arguments are just part of living with someone else. You will annoy each other, so deal with it. I know that if you ask my husband, he'll tell you I am a pain in the behind to live with when my writing is giving me problems. Nobody is perfect, and we all have our little quirks. Honestly, marriage (or any long-term relationship) is a job that needs to be tackled one day at a time. There will be good times and tough times. How you deal with them defines who you are, both as an individual and as a couple.

So, for those days when you are on each other's last nerve and you both need to sweeten up your dispositions, try this sweet tongue-in-cheek spell for bad days.

A Sweet Spell for a Bad Day

Supplies

- A small, pink, rose-scented candle (rose scent for love, and the pink color to encourage soft emotions)

- A candle holder

- A few drops of honey (to sweeten up the situation)

- Matches or a lighter

- Your love altar

- A photo of the two of you

Directions

Work this spell as needed. If you can time it out to a Friday or catch a waning moon, fantastic. If not, well, your intention to create change is the greatest tool of magick you possess. If you need to get the spell going right now, then by all means, work it.

To begin this spell, rub a few drops of the honey along the sides and top of the pink candle. Technically, this is referred to as "dressing" the candle. Once that is done, place the pink candle in the holder. Wash your hands, if necessary. Set up the photo in front of the candle in the holder. In your mind's eye, see the silly argument and focus on the aggravation or the anger that you feel because of it.

Now, realistically, just how important is this argument, anyway? In the grand scheme of things, will the world stop revolving? Is it worth carrying on a battle over it? Once you have thought about it and start to calm down, visualize that the problem and any negativity that was built are slowly fading away. When you feel calmer, light the pink spell candle and repeat the spell verse three times:

With this magick spell, while roses scent the air,
Let us settle our feud in a way that's fair.
You're a grumpy guy, and I'm a pissy Witch,
From sour to sweet, our attitudes will switch.
As the candle burns away, we will unify,
Now let's make up and kiss our troubles goodbye.

Close up the spell with these lines:

By scent, flame, and honey, this spell is done,
For the good of all, bringing harm to none.

Allow the candle to burn in a safe place until it goes out on its own. Now go find your man and make nice. Or, if he is the one who apologizes, then accept it graciously. Kiss and make up. (Afterwards, you could always indulge in a little make-up sex.)

How to Disenchant a Man
Breaking a Love Spell Gone Sour

Oh, oh, Rhett. For the first time I'm finding out
what it is to be sorry for something I've done.

Scarlett O'Hara, Gone with the Wind

Oh no, tell me you didn't. You did not go ahead and cast a love spell on a specific target, did you? Or you went ahead and cast a spell while you were emotionally distraught? Well, crap. So now, instead of an adoring love slave, you've got an obsessive or violent stalker-type man in your life. Or perhaps you have enjoyed the worst run of luck imaginable since you cast that spell.

Hmm . . . I smell karma.

Well, girlfriend, now you've done it, and now it's up to you to un-do it. For those of you who jumped to this part of the book first, brace yourselves; you are about to get a lecture. For those of you who are merrily reading along, settle in and pay attention; this information is still good for you to have.

Why did I warn you against this sort of thing early on in the book? Because manipulative love spells or the classic "I'll-get-even-with-you" types of spells literally open up a floodgate of trouble. All you can do is get the hell out of the way and scramble for higher ground. The spell will have to run its course, and it may take a few weeks. However, now that you are clinging to the ledge, wondering if you have climbed high enough to get out of harm's way, I suggest you really think back and remember exactly what you did to start this whole mess. If you want to turn the tide, then you need to be

the dark side of love

♥

proactive and do something to help reverse the manipulative and negative energy that your spell unleashed. You can't just sit and pray to the Goddess about how sorry you are and wait for it to pass. No, ma'am. You need to get in there and start working to make amends and repair the damage.

In truth, affirmative magick requires self-control, kindness, and compassion. So now that you have learned a rather painful lesson, you better dig down deep and apply that consideration in your everyday life from now on. I bet you'll think twice now before you cast any other borderline spells, and I'll bet you will make damn sure you are indeed working for the good of all.

When you need to work magick to reverse the energies that an earlier spell has caused, this is technically referred to as a reversal, or an uncrossing. An uncrossing focuses on removing the effects of a hex or any manipulative or malignant spell. And here is how you do it.

An Uncrossing Ritual

So, if you showed poor judgment and now have a situation on your hands, it's time to admit your mistake. Taking responsibility for your actions and acknowledging the lesson you have learned is a first positive step in the right direction. Read this spell before you work it. There is a lot to do, and it is involved. Take your time and study it so the uncrossing ritual goes smoothly.

Supplies

- A sheet of paper and a black pen

- Quick-drying white correction fluid, or white paint and a small brush

- 12 inches of white ribbon

- A gray candle (to neutralize the effects of the original spell)

- A candle holder (for the gray candle)

- A black taper candle (it needs to be a taper—you will be breaking it in half during the ritual)

- An uncrossing herb/plant, such as dried hydrangea flowers, dried chamomile, or small twigs from an elm tree (work with whatever botanicals you can easily procure)

- 1 cup salt

- A resealable freezer bag

- A lighter or matches

Timing

The best time to work this uncrossing would be during a waning moon phase: as the moon wanes, so will the problems. However, if you do not have the luxury of waiting a few weeks for the correct moon phase, then I recommend working on a Saturday, as Saturdays are perfect days to banish problems.

Directions

Set up this uncrossing ritual wherever you worked the original spell that caused so many problems. Take a hard look at the original spell that you worked. Can you see where your problems started? Did you target someone specifically? Were negative emotions involved, or was the original spell manipulative? Did you change it around or reword it? What exactly did you do? Think about it, and figure out where you went wrong.

To begin the ritual, light the gray candle and ask the Goddess in your own words for her assistance. With the black pen, write down the original spell that you performed on a piece of paper, and set it aside. Next, take the correction fluid, or the white paint, and draw a large white *X* over the middle of the original spell. As you do so, say out loud:

I neutralize any harm that I have caused.
As I will it, then so must it be.

Set aside the correction fluid/paint. Give the paper a moment or two to dry. Now carefully roll up that crossed-out spell into a tight roll of paper (roll the spell to the inside of the scroll). Secure it closed with the white ribbon. Knot the ribbon three times, and say:

By the power of three times three,
I neutralize all negativity.

Now place the rolled-up spell into the freezer bag. Add the uncrossing herbs. As you slowly pour the salt on top of the scroll of paper, say these lines:

May the salt and herbs now create a reverse,
And protect us both from any further curse.

Set the bag aside, but keep it in easy reach. Take the black taper and light it, using the flame from the gray candle. Hold the taper in your hands and let it burn for a few moments. (The black taper represents the original spell.) Now speak the following lines:

A love conjured is a false love, and now I cast it away,
The love magick I cast on (name) is neutralized today.
A hard lesson has been learned, and now I make amends,
Any trouble my spell has caused now comes to an end.

Pinch out the taper candle and snap it in half. Make sure the wick is completely extinguished, then place it also inside the freezer bag, flatten out the bag, and zip it closed. Visualize the other person as free, healthy, and happy. Wish them well and out of your life. Be sincere.

Close up the ritual by saying:

Uncrossed you'll now forever be,
This ritual has set you free.

Allow the gray candle to burn in a safe place until it goes out on its own; just be sure to keep an eye on it. Now gather up the freezer bag and dispose of it in a public garbage can that is well away from where you live and work. Once you have disposed of the bag, turn your back and walk away. Do not look back. Put all this behind you, and move on to better things.

the dark side of love

♥

Breaking Up and Moving On

Now I will tell you what I've done for you
50,000 tears I cry
Screaming, deceiving, and bleeding for you
And you still won't hear me ...

Amy Lee, David Hodges & Ben Moody, "Going Under"

Sometimes breaking up and moving on is the very best thing you can do. It is neither easy nor pleasant; however, if you've got a cheating partner, are in an emotionally unhealthy or unstable relationship, or (Goddess forbid) an abusive relationship, it is the smartest move you can make. Oh, and let me say right here and now: if you have found yourself in a physically abusive relationship, you don't need a Witch. You need the police, a lawyer, and counseling. Get out. Get your children out, go to a shelter, call the police, and report the abuse. Start taking the first steps to reclaiming a healthier and violence-free life.

When a relationship falls apart, it is tough, no matter who you are. Sometimes it's a relief and sometimes it's a heartbreaker. Either way, it's going to be a cathartic event. Once the emotional storm has passed and you begin to get back into the swing of things, you will feel the need to put all the emotional baggage behind you.

Begin the process by getting rid of mementos from the old relationship. If you have wedding jewelry, you have a couple of options: you can sell the jewelry or take it to a jeweler and have it made into something else. Also remember to toss out old cards and photos, and literally clean house. The following ritual will help you when you are ready to begin to move on.

The Elemental "Moving Forward" Ritual

Timing

The best time to work this ritual is on the day of the new moon. This is a perfect time, as the moon is dark but slowly increasing toward the light. It represents how you are moving on and moving forward. Alternately, you could work this spell on a Saturday at sunset. If you choose this time, you will tap into the closing energies of the day and of the week. This ritual will take a bit of time, so read over the directions before you begin.

Supplies

- A white tealight candle

- Matches or a lighter

- A small bowl of water

- A turquoise stone (for healing)

- A fallen feather

- A photo of the two of you

- A white envelope

- A 12-inch length of white ribbon

- A green organza favor bag or a 4-inch square of green material and enough ribbon to tie the fabric closed into a small pouch

- One stick of sandalwood incense (for cleansing)

- An incense holder

- Your love altar or a safe, flat work surface

Directions

This spell employs the power of the four elements. They are represented in the spell by the candle flame for fire, the feather for air, the tumbled turquoise stone for earth, and lastly the bowl of water. To begin this spell, take a ritual bath. Sprinkle a bit of salt in the water for its cleansing purposes, or pour in some scented bubble bath and have a nice therapeutic soak in the tub. Once the water cools, step out of the tub, dry off, and put on a clean robe or clean clothes. (If you don't care for a tub bath, then take a nice, cleansing shower. Lather up with your favorite soap or scented shower gel, and as the water pours down on you, visualize it washing away any worries.)

When you begin the actual spell, arrange the components to your liking on your work area. To begin, pick up the bowl of water. Bless the water with this line:

By my words, this water is blessed;
It brings happiness, joy, and success.

Set the water back on your work surface. Now light the tealight candle, and say:

By the element of fire,
This situation begins to transform.

Take a few moments to center yourself. Be calm, and think of positive things and your new, happier future. Repeat the verse below:

The emotional bond between us is broken,
Dispelling pain or guilt as the charm is spoken.
The love that was between us shall now transform,
Allowing new relationships to be born.

Now take the photo of the two of you and carefully tear it in two. Don't just rip it in half, separate your images. Set them apart on your workspace, and say:

Once joined as one, we are now apart.
Freedom to both by this Witch's art.

Take the image of your old lover and bind the feather to it with the white ribbon while saying:

May the element of air blow in new opportunities for you.

Or, depending on the situation, you might wish to say instead:

May the element of air speed you far away from me.

the dark side of love

♥

Place the photo and the feather in the envelope. Set it aside. Now, put your image and the turquoise stone together into the green charm bag. As you slip the stone and your photo into the bag, or tie up the edges of the fabric around it, say:

May the element of earth help me to heal and to be strong.

Take the blessed water from the bowl, dip your fingers in it, and put a drop of it on your chest, right over your heart. Visualize it washing away old hurts and sorrows. Now take that bowl of water and sprinkle a bit with your fingertips at each of the corners of your home. As you do, you can say:

By the power of water, I wash away all negativity.

The tealight candle will burn for approximately four hours. When it goes out, neatly dispose of the little candle cup and the envelope. After you have done so, light the sandalwood incense and carry the smoking incense around your home. Go to every room and wave the smoke gently around.

This smudging technique is a final clearing-out of any old hurt feelings or sour vibrations. Wave a bit of the scented smoke over yourself as well. Once the incense has burned out, go back to your altar. Close up the ritual with these lines:

Once joined as one, we are now apart.
Freedom to both by this Witch's art.
By the elements four, this healing spell is done,
For the good of all and bringing harm to no one.

A Few Witchy Words of Wisdom

I was always thought to be "stuck up."

I wasn't—I was sure of myself.

This is and always has been an unforgivable quality to the unsure.

Bette Davis

I hope that the spells and rituals in this chapter will be helpful to you. Remember that even the darkest night eventually gives way to the dawn. So stand tough and work your way through any romantic problems that you may face. Use your inherent bewitching qualities as a woman and rise above troubles and dramas with style, strength, humor, and wisdom. Be sure of yourself and who you are. You can do it, and you can do it well.

I believe in you.

A Woman's Witchery

Who were the witches, where did they come from?
Maybe your great, great grandmother was one.
Witches were wise, wise women they say,
And there's a little witch in every woman today.

Bonnie Lockhart, "The Witch Song"

hope that you have enjoyed your journey into the mystical, magickal world of enchantments. Women are by their very nature "bewitching" creatures. Remember that the main components to all magick are an open, loving heart and the desire to make a positive change. Your intentions and emotions actually do fuel your magick, so a tender heart, your feminine intuition, a sense of humor, and compassion are all important tools for you to keep nearby.

I imagine that a bit of time has passed since you first started reading this book. Along the way, you have experimented and tried your hand at the enchantments and charms, and you have experienced magick at work within your life. A whole new world has opened up in front of your eyes, and whether you are an old hand at the Craft or a newcomer, it is always a thrill to learn something new and to stretch your talents.

To live is to learn, and as we travel along our own individual paths, we will have many opportunities to experience love and to gain knowledge. There is a wise and loving enchantress inside of every woman. Let her out, and watch her play. See what she teaches you and what wonderful, positive changes are created within your life.

May your path be filled with joy and passion, light, laughter, and love . . . and, of course, magick.

Happy spellcrafting, and blessed be!

Ellen Dugan

Passionate Potpourri

And yet for all this help of head and brain
How happily instinctive we remain,
Our best guide upward further to the light,
Passionate preference such as love at sight.

Robert Frost

his appendix covers a bit of this and a bit of that. It is a colorful
mixture of coordinating magickal objects that all promote love,
such as crystals, flowers, and herbs. These tips and tricks will come
in handy when you are designing your own spells. There is information on love gods
and goddesses from many different cultures and traditions, and a spell worksheet for
you to make copies of and work with.

All of the corresponding information in this appendix is here for you to experiment with and to add to your loving enchantments. Try adding a complementary crystal, flower, or herb to personalize the spells and charms that you have found in this book. Take a look at the list of deities who specialize in love and romance. Try calling on them, and see what sort of difference you experience in your magick.

Designing Your Own Enchantments

You have witchcraft in your lips, Kate.

Shakespeare, Henry V

The following suggested natural items, symbols, and deities are complementary to love magick and loving enchantments. If you are already well versed in magick, you may have your own correspondences and preferences, and by all means go with your favorite herbs, stones, or flowers. However, if you'd like to learn something new, or if this is all new to you, then this list of corresponding items will come in handy as you begin to design your own enchantments.

In the following indexes, I list easy to acquire herbs and flowers. The flowers may be harvested from your own garden or purchased from the neighborhood florist. The crystals and stones are easy to locate at a nature-themed store, a metaphysical shop, or the local magickal store. Tumbled stones are usually inexpensive and cost about a dollar or so. On my altar at home, I keep a pretty blue star-shaped dish full of various tumbled stones. That way, they are handy for any charms, spells, or rituals I care to conjure up.

Thirteen Stones for Love

We love because it is the only true adventure.

Nikki Giovanni

When choosing a stone for any type of spellwork, hold the stone in your receptive hand (the opposite hand from the one you write with). Close your eyes and call upon your intuitive powers. With your eyes closed, gather your impressions about the stone. Does it feel warm? Did it give you a little tingle? Trust your own instincts, and select your stones carefully. Take your time choosing and purchasing a few good stones to work with, and enjoy the process.

Agate: The agate is a healing and love-promoting stone. Agates come in many colors and varieties; see which ones feel the best to you.

Amber: This is actually a resin. This golden "stone" attracts love and prosperity and strengthens any magick. It is sacred to the goddess Freya. Amber will hold an electrical charge, and it enhances your inner beauty and can be used to promote fertility.

Amethyst: A wonderful all-purpose purple stone. The amethyst is a calming and peaceful stone. It relieves stress and promotes spirituality. It sharpens psychic abilities and also is a good love stone when set into jewelry exchanged between lovers.

Carnelian: This red stone is thought to prevent anger and jealousy. It nullifies bad feelings, resentment, and hatred, so it would be a good addition to several of the spells in chapter 8. This stone restores self-confidence and gives your courage a lift. It also stimulates sexuality and can boost the libido.

Garnet: A gorgeous deep burgundy-colored semi-precious gemstone, garnet brings extra energy, helps strengthen the body, and boosts your personal power. Carrying the stones will increase your confidence, and it pulls romance and love into your life. (See the garnet jewelry charm in chapter 6.)

Lapis lazuli: This gorgeous deep-blue stone promotes spirituality, protection, psychic abilities, faithfulness, and love. It is associated with the goddess Isis. Lapis lazuli is rumored to be an excellent aid in keeping a lover faithful, and it can also be used to strengthen a loving bond between a married couple or a solid, established relationship.

Malachite: This lovely, banded green stone is a favorite of mine. It has many uses, including protection, prosperity, peace, and, of course, love. Holding a malachite stone in your hand will increase your ability to draw love into your life and be more loving to others.

Moonstone: A feminine stone that encourages empathy, love, safe travel, psychic abilities, and moon magick. Moonstone jewelry set in silver is very popular with Witches and Goddess worshipers for ritual necklaces, rings, and earrings. This stone is traditionally sacred to the moon goddess. If you wear or carry moonstones on your person, you can draw love into your life. Moonstones will also increase your sensitivity to other people's moods, hidden feelings, and emotions. Moonstones exchanged between squabbling partners are said to help end their feud, encourage love again, and help heal the troubled relationship.

Pearl: The pearl is associated with the moon and the Goddess. It is worked into spells for love and abundance and is sacred to many goddesses, including Aphrodite, Diana, Venus, and the Hindu goddess Lakshmi. According to Hindu mythology, the tradition of brides wearing pearls began when the god Krishna gave his daughter pearls to wear on her wedding day. It is interesting to note that women in India traditionally wear pearls to magickally ensure a happy marriage.

Rose quartz: This soft rose-pink crystal is the ultimate "warm fuzzy" stone. Rose quartz can open up your heart and is used to draw love into your life. This stone also encourages self-love. Try stringing rose quartz beads into a bracelet to promote love and to encourage its energies in your life. (See chapter 6 for this bracelet spell and the directions.) This stone also promotes peace, contentment, and faithfulness in marriages and long-term relationships.

Tourmaline, pink: Tourmaline comes in several colors, and this particular shade of stone pulls in love and companionship. It can also make you more sensitive to other people and their needs and feelings.

Tourmaline, watermelon: This stone looks like it sounds, with bands of green, white, and pink in the stone. It helps you get in touch with both sides of your personality, the strong warrior and the gentle nurturer, the active and the intuitive. This stone is also used to draw love into your life.

Turquoise: This is a wonderful protective and healing stone. It also is a symbol of married love, friendship, and affection. Turquoise is thought to be especially powerful if it is exchanged between two lovers.

Herbs and Flowers for Love

Flowers … are a proud assertion that a ray of beauty
Outvalues all the utilities of the world.

Ralph Waldo Emerson

Here are some common herbs, blooming shrubs, and enchanting flowers to add to your love spells, charms, and rituals. Some of these botanicals were featured in the chapter's spells and charms, and some are here to spark your imagination and get your creativity flowing.

Azalea, white: The blossoms of the azalea represent a first love.

Basil: The scent of this popular herb can cause sympathy between two people. It also helps to keep your lover true. According to folklore, if a man accepts a basil plant from a woman, he will love her forever.

Butterfly bush: These fragrant blossoms encourage wantonness. They would be wonderful to incorporate into passion-inducing spells (or to encourage a little bodice-ripping).

Carnation: The carnation is associated with the element of fire and brings energy to your spellwork. The flower itself symbolizes a pure and passionate love. Take a look at chapter 6 for more information on the magickal colors of the carnation and more ideas for designing your own spells and charms.

Catnip: This herb is linked to the element of water. This plant is, as you'd expect, sacred to the Egyptian cat-headed goddess Bast, and it may be added to spells to encourage a sense of playfulness and passion.

Daisy: This flower brings sweetness, innocence, and simplicity. Also associated with the love goddess Freya, the daisy can be worked into spells for love and passion.

Dill: This herb is associated with the element of fire. The scent of this herb is thought to induce lust. Dill is also protective and encourages prosperity to boot.

Feverfew: This gorgeous blooming herb is linked to the element of water. It grows well in the home herb garden and looks like miniature white daisies. It is a popular magickal plant for healing, and in the language of flowers it means "flirtation."

Geranium, white: In the language of flowers, it represents gracefulness. According to flower folklore, it encourages fertility.

Hydrangea: This shrub's protective blossoms are used in uncrossing spells.

Ivy: This is a feminine plant, according to plant folklore. It is tucked into wedding bouquets to grant the bride good luck, and it also represents wedded love and fidelity.

Lavender: This fragrant herb is associated with the element of air. It is a classic ingredient in love sachets and charm bags that promote luck, affection, and romance (see chapter 6 for a lavender love sachet recipe). This herb is easy to grow in a sunny garden at home and is readily available at arts and crafts stores in the dried flower section.

Lilac: Lilac blossoms are sacred to the nature spirits and loved by the faerie kingdom. In the language of flowers, purple lilac blossoms symbolize a first, true love, while white lilacs represent purity and sweetness.

Myrtle: This blooming shrub is sacred to Aphrodite and Venus. The myrtle is associated with the element of water and induces love, passion, faithfulness, and connubial happiness.

Orchid: In the language of flowers, the orchid announces the qualities of beauty, luxury, and refinement, which explains why they have been so popular as bridal flowers. A traditional component in old love spells, orchid blossoms are also rumored to induce lust.

Pansy: This cheerful flower is sacred to Eros. The story goes that Eros accidentally hit the pansy with one of his love-inducing arrows, and forever after the flower "smiled" its pleasure. The pansy, also known as the viola, has the elemental correspondence of water. According to folklore, its happy face eases a broken heart. In the language of flowers, it encourages loving thoughts. It also demands that you "think of me."

Peony: In the language of flowers, the peony nods to a bashful love. Magickally, it is a very protective flower. Place vases of peony flowers about the home to enforce protective vibrations and to chase away nightmares.

Rose: The classic flower for love spells and charms. Sacred to many love deities, the rose is romantic and represents beauty, love, and romance. The various colors of the rose have separate magickal meanings. **Red:** true love. **Red and white:** creativity, camaraderie, and marriage. **Pale pink:** a first tender and romantic love. **Hot pink:** a contemporary love full of energy and enthusiasm. **Orange:** vitality, ardor, and verve. **Yellow:** friendship and sunshine. **Pale green:** fertility, prosperity, and good luck. **Blue:** miracles. **Purple:** passion and power. **Burgundy:** a dark, tempestuous love. **White:** peace, love, and moon magick. **Ivory:** a mature and steadfast love.

Rosemary: This herb is linked to the element of fire. It carries the message to "remember me." In the language of flowers, rosemary symbolizes devotion and faithfulness. It is a classic addition to love sachets and charm bags.

Tulips: This flower corresponds with the element of earth. It represents prosperity and fame and announces that you are a perfect lover. See chapter 6 for a list of the tulip's magickal color associations.

Violet: According to flower languages, the violet symbolizes modesty and simplicity. It also conveys the message that "I love you, too!" Violets are sacred to the faerie kingdom. On an interesting note, all blue flowers are adored by the love goddesses Aphrodite and Venus, and if you incorporate blue flowers in your love spells, you will surely grant their favors.

Yarrow: This all-purpose blooming herb is a favorite magickal plant. It has the elemental association of water and can be used for any magickal purpose you could imagine. Yarrow has the power to keep a couple happily together for seven years. It is easy to grow in a sunny garden at home and is readily available in arts and crafts stores in the dried flower section.

Love Gods and Goddesses

And the Goddess?
She stands
Between the worlds.

Denise Levertov

Here is a bit of information about various gods and goddesses of love and passion. Their origin is listed, as well as any associated candle colors, symbols or other information that can be used when working with the particular deity. Try carving their symbol onto a spell candle or arranging your altar around a replica of the deity. Search the Internet for a picture of them to print. Always use your imagination and personalize your spellcraft.

Aphrodite (Greek): A mother goddess of passionate love and desire. Aphrodite can help you feel more confident in your own skin and with your sexuality. Her symbols include the seashell, the rose, pearls, coral, and the ocean, and her colors are aqua and pink.

Astarte (Phoenician): Goddess of the moon, love, and fertility. Her symbol is the waxing crescent moon in the dusky western sky. Her colors are rose and silver.

Bast (Egyptian): The beautiful cat-headed goddess. Bast is associated with love, joy, music, sexuality, and fertility. Her symbols are black cats, all domestic cats, and the sistrum. Her colors are green and black.

Brigit (Celtic): A goddess of healing, fire, inspiration, and poetry. Symbols include a flame, the cauldron, and the hearth. Brigit is the goddess to call on for matters of emotional healing, to encourage domestic bliss, and for the sanctity of hearth and home. Her colors are red and white.

Diana (Greco-Roman): A lunar goddess and a significant deity for Witches and contemporary Goddess worshippers. Diana is a patron for outspoken, strong-willed, and courageous women. She can help you find the courage to walk your own unique path in life. Diana is fearless and wise. Symbols for her include the waxing crescent moon, the full moon, and a bow and quiver full of arrows. Her traditional colors are silver and white.

Eros (Greek): The ancient, winged fertility god of erotic love and sexual relations. Eros is sometimes confused with a modern depiction of the baby Cupid. However, this is an ancient deity and one of the first to come into the world, even before the Olympians. Picture Eros as a handsome and virile man—think of a romance book-cover type of guy. Eros was married to Psyche and was considered to be the most loved and the most loving of the Greek gods. His symbols are a bow, golden arrows, and wings. His sacred color is red.

Frey (Norse): A god of fertility and male potency, Frey is the brother of Freya. He is associated with virility, pleasure, peace, sensual love, joy, and beauty. His sacred animal is the boar. His color is green.

Freya (Norse): Goddess of love, beauty, sex, and visionary magick. Freya was especially gifted in spellcraft. Her magickal associations include the gemstone amber, domestic and wild cats, the primrose, and strawberries. Her colors are green, red, and black.

Hathor (Egyptian): Horned goddess of beauty, fertility, and music. The cow, mirrors, and a solar disc are her symbols. Her color is sky blue.

Hecate (Greek): The goddess of the crossroads and protector of all Witches. A lunar goddess with many titles, including the Queen of the Night. Hecate is a mistress of magick and has many faces and guises. She may appear as an enchanting maiden, a bewitching matron, or a wise crone. She is a deity of magick and spellcraft, and her magickal symbols include dogs, the cauldron, a burning torch, keys, and three-way crossings. Her colors are black and silver.

Hestia (Greek): The goddess of the heart and of the home. Hestia is the spirit of the hearth fire. She was the first of all Greek gods to be invoked, as she embodied the living flame at the center of the earth. Call on Hestia for family love and unity, as she is a protector of the home and of the family. Her sacred color is flame red.

Innana (Sumerian): Innana is a lunar goddess of fertility, love, and battle. Her symbols are the chariot and lions, and her color is red.

Ishtar (Babylonian): Also known as the Queen of Heaven, this is an ancient and powerful goddess of love, procreation, and war. Her symbols are the slim, new crescent moon in the western sky and the planet Venus shining in the heavens. Jewelry, such as bracelets, necklaces, and rings, corresponds with this deity, as she is typically depicted wearing many pieces of jewelry. Her colors are red and green.

Isis (Egyptian): The supreme goddess of love, marriage, fertility, and magick, Isis was worshipped all over the world for thousands of years. She is a powerful archetype to call upon. One of her titles is the Goddess of Ten Thousand Names. Isis is the beautiful winged goddess, the loving wife of Osiris, and the mother of Horus. Her color is deep blue, her sacred stone is lapis lazuli, and her symbols include the throne (which is the hieroglyph for her name), golden wings, the sun, and the moon.

Juno (Roman): The Roman personification of the Great Mother. Juno is the matriarch and the patron and protector of married women and children. Her symbols include the peacock, figs, and coins. Her colors are silver and peacock blue.

Kuan Yin (Chinese): The goddess of compassion, mercy, kindness, fertility, and childbirth. As a mother goddess, she is associated with the full moon. Her symbols include birds and the willow branch. Her color is white.

Lakshmi (India): The four-armed goddess of beauty and prosperity. Grace and charm are the gifts of this deity. Her sacred animal is the elephant, and her symbols include the lotus, pearls, and gold coins. Her sacred colors are gold and red.

Lilith (Sumerian): The winged goddess of lust, sexuality, and desire. Lilith is the dangerous seductress, the beautiful vampire, and the ultimate femme fatale. Her symbols include midnight-colored wings; dark red, thorny roses; and owls. Her colors are deep burgundy, blood red, and black.

Pan (Greek): The goat-footed god Pan is a lusty and rowdy god of the forests and woods who is often depicted as a robust man with the legs, horns, and ears of a goat. Pan had an eye for the ladies, was a real party animal, and was always on the prowl. He represents the joy of the physical act of love, the unbridled force of sexuality, and the drive to procreate. Symbols that are sacred to Pan are pan pipes, fresh foliage and greenery, and any wild place in nature. His color is forest green.

Selene (Greek): Selene is the beautiful goddess of the full moon. Selene is especially fond of Witches and magick users in general. She is known for her quick responses and practical magickal solutions. Selene is classically depicted as a pale-faced woman crowned with a crescent moon. All night-blooming flowers fall under her auspices. Her sacred flower is the bluebell. Selene's colors are white, silver, and blue.

Yemaya (African/Caribbean): Yemaya is also called the Star of the Seven Seas and is sometimes depicted as a beautiful black mermaid. Her magick includes love, comfort, and bringing life-giving rains to the land. Women and children are under her protection. Her colors are white, ocean blue, and sea green. Symbols for her include dolphins, seashells, and mermaids. According to tradition, Yemaya likes offerings of fresh melons and white and blue glass beads. If you call upon Yemaya, be sure to leave her a gift of one of those items to gain her favor.

Spell Worksheet

Oh, you smile, you smile
And then the spell was cast
And here we are in heaven
For you are mine at last.

M. Gordon & H. Warren, "At Last"

When I draft my own spells and charms, I have found it easiest to work from a worksheet. Here is one for you to copy and use. This is a wonderful tool to help you organize your supplies, calculate lunar timing, draft your spell verses, and plot out your best course of magickal action. Brightest blessings on your spellwork!

Goal: _____

_____

_____

Moon Phase: _____

_____

_____

Day of the Week: _____

_____

_____

Astrological / Magickal Symbols Used: _____

_____

_____

Deity Invoked: _____

_____

_____

Candle Color (if you added candle magick): _____

_____

_____

Herbs or Flowers Used: _____

_____

_____

Magickal Significance of the Flowers / Herbs: _____

_____

_____

Crystals or Stones Used and Their Associations: _____

_____

_____

Charm or Verse: _____

_____

_____

Results: _____

_____

_____

_____

_____

_____

Glossary

Words, words, mere words, no matter from the heart.

Shakespeare

Amulet: A type of herbal charm, ornament, or jewel that aids or protects its wearer.

Autumn equinox: One of the eight Witch's sabbats. The festival date changes from year to year, depending on when the sun enters the astrological sign of Libra (approximately September 21–23). The autumn equinox, also known as Mabon, is, at its core, a harvest festival and a time of balance and plenty. Colors for this fall festival include those fall shades of red, brown, orange, gold, and yellow. Symbols for this sabbat include corn stalks, pumpkins, ornamental corn, fall foliage, the apple, and the overflowing cornucopia.

Banishing: Repelling an unwanted person or negative situation.

Beltane: One of the eight sabbats, Beltane begins at sundown on April 30. May 1 is Beltane Day, or May Day. Beltane is celebrated with flowers, feasting, dancing, and maypoles. This is a lusty sabbat, it marks the halfway point between spring and summer, and it is a prime time to encounter the faeries. A good time to work spells for passion and romance. Colors include bright shades of hot pink, purple, yellow, peach, blue, and green, or the more traditional red and white.

Charm: A rhyming series of words (a simple spell) used for a specific magickal purpose. Also see amulet.

Charm bag: Similar to a sachet, a charm bag is a small cloth bag filled with aromatic herbs, charged crystals, and other magickal ingredients. Charm bags can be carried for a variety of magickal reasons, such as to promote love, healing, protection, or prosperity.

Craft, the: The Witches' term for the Old Religion and practice of Witchcraft.

Dressing: This refers to the act of anointing a candle or another magickal object or tool with a substance such as essential oil, spring water, or honey.

Elements: The four natural elements are earth, air, fire, and water.

Enchant: The classic definitions are 1. To sing to. 2. To influence by or as if by charms and incantation; bewitch. 3. To attract and move deeply; rouse to ecstatic admiration.

Ethics: If you don't know what these are, you are in big trouble. Refer to the definitions of Harm none and Wiccan Rede.

Florigraphy: The language of flowers.

Flower fascination: Fascination is the art of directing another's consciousness or will toward you, to command or bewitch. Flower fascinations are elementary flower spells and floral charms used for various magickal purposes.

Grounding and centering: This is a visualization technique, a way to focus and relax before or after performing magick. You push negativity and stress away from your own body, calming and focusing on your center.

Harm none: This is a promise and an oath to never harm any living thing with the use of magick or personal power. You have no doubt noticed the use of this phrase throughout the book: For the good of all, bringing harm to none. (Also refer to the Wiccan Rede.)

Herbalism: The use of herbs in conjunction with magick to bring about a positive change.

Imbolc: One of the eight sabbats, Imbolc is the halfway point between winter and spring that is traditionally celebrated on February 2. If you look carefully at nature at that time, you will see signs of winter loosening its grip on the land. This day is also known as Candlemas and Groundhog Day. Symbols for this sabbat include snow and ice, the purple crocus, snowdrops, white candles, and the four-spoked Brigit's cross.

Invoke: The drawing of a beloved deity's essence into your own body, allowing the deity to temporarily channel its powers, personality, and wisdom through you. (For example, asking Aphrodite to lend her passion and loving qualities to you for a time.) This is a willing act and one of ultimate love and trust.

Lammas: One of the eight sabbats, this festival of the first harvest is celebrated on August 1. At this time, the first of the field and vegetable crops are harvested. This festival occurs at the height of summer when the temperatures are extreme. Colors are gold, yellow, and green. Symbols for this sabbat include garden vegetables, summer fruits and berries, ears of corn, the sunflower, and sheaves of wheat.

Law of Three: A traditional rule of the Craft and positive magick that states "ever mind the rule of three, three times what thou givest returns to thee." This is a lesson in cause and effect, meaning that whatever type of magickal energy you send out into the world, it will be returned to you in kind times three.

Magick: This is the art and science of creating positive change in your life. Magick is a force of nature and a sympathetic process. It works in harmony with your own personal power and the elements of nature—earth, air, fire, and water—to bring loving and constructive transformation into your life.

Midsummer: The summer solstice and another sabbat. Midsummer is celebrated on or around June 21. The summer solstice is the peak of the sun's power and strength. This is our longest day and shortest night. From this point on, the sunlight hours will slowly decrease until the winter solstice in December. Midsummer is an opportune time to work garden magick and to work with the faeries. Colors to work with are green and gold. The natural symbols of fresh flowers and green leaves from the garden are most appropriate.

Natural magician: A magickal practitioner who works mainly with simple earthy supplies, the four elements, and in harmony with herbs and nature.

Nosegay: A small floral bouquet, typically round in shape. Also called a tussie-mussie.

Ostara: The vernal equinox and a sabbat that falls on or around March 21. This festival day is named after a Norse goddess of spring, Eostre. Daylight and nighttime hours are equal on this day. This spring festival celebrates light and life returning to the earth, and is a time for fresh starts and plans for the future. Colors for this sabbat are pastel shades of pink, baby blue, pale yellow and green, soft lilac, and spring green. Symbols for this festival include dyed eggs, spring flowers, and Eostre's sacred rabbit.

Ritual: An involved, more formal act of magick, usually containing a spell and other specific acts. Rituals typically take longer to perform, have many steps, are more involved, and are more intense and serious in nature.

Sabbat: One of the eight solar festivals, or holidays, celebrated by Pagan religions. The sabbats include Imbolc, Ostara, Beltane, Midsummer, Lammas, Mabon, Samhain, and Yule.

Samhain: This sabbat is also known as the Celtic New Year and Halloween, and is celebrated at sundown on October 31. On this day, the veil between the spirit world and the physical world is at its thinnest. This popular holiday is an excellent time to perform love divination, and it is traditionally used to honor the memories of any loved ones who have passed over. Colors for this sabbat include orange and black. Symbols for this festival include the pumpkin, jack-o'-lanterns, and fall foliage.

Smudging: This is the act of passing a person or object through the smoke of a purifying incense, such as lavender, sandalwood, sage, or frankincense. When the smoke passes over your body or an object, it removes negativity, sour energy, and negative vibrations.

Spell: A specific act of magick that creates positive change in agreement with your own will, wishes, and desires.

Tag line: A tag line is a few closing lines that you "tag" onto the end of a spell to ensure that the magick is nonmanipulative and for the free will and the good of all.

Triple Moon Goddess: Refers to the three faces of the Goddess: the Maiden is symbolized by the waxing moon, the Mother is represented by the full moon, and the Crone is honored with the waning moon.

Uncrossing Ritual: A magickal act that focuses on removing the effects of a hex or any manipulative spell (see chapter 8, pages 184–187).

Wicca: The contemporary name for the religion of the Witch. Wicca takes its roots from the Anglo-Saxon word *wicce*, which may mean "wise." It is also thought to mean "to shape or to bend." Wicca is a Pagan religion based on the cycles of nature and the belief in karma, reincarnation, and the worship of both a god and a goddess.

Wiccan Rede: The absolute rule that Wiccans, Witches, and magicians ethically live by. The Rede states simply, "An' it harm none, do what you will."

Yule: The sabbat that falls on the winter solstice, celebrated on or around December 21. The winter solstice is the shortest day and the longest night of the year. Yule is traditionally a time when Pagans celebrate the Mother Goddess and the return of the newly born Sun King, who is sometimes referred to as the Child of Light. Colors for this sabbat are red, green, white, and gold. Gift giving, decorated trees, the Yule log, fresh holly, mistletoe, and evergreen wreaths feature prominently in Yule celebrations.

Bibliography

Books let us into their souls and lay open
to us the secrets of our own.

William Hazlitt

Almond, Jocelyn, and Keith Seddon. *Understanding the Tarot*. London: Aquarian
  Press, 1991.

Arkins, Diane C. *Halloween Merrymaking.* Gretna, LA: Pelican Publishing Company,
  2004.

Bartlett, Sarah. *Feng Shui for Lovers*. New York: Kondansha America, 1999.

Biziou, Barbara. *The Joy of Ritual.* New York: Golden Books, 1999.

Bowes, Susan. *Notions and Potions.* New York: Sterling Publishing Company, 1997.

Cabot, Laurie, and Tom Cowan. *Love Magic*. New York: Dell Publishing Company, 1992.

Cabot, Laurie, and Jean Mills. *Celebrate the Earth: A Year of Holidays in the Pagan Tradition*. New York: Dell Publishing Company, 1994.

————. *The Witch in Every Woman*. New York: Dell Publishing Company, 1997.

Clark, Stacy, M.A., and Eve Adamson. *The Complete Idiot's Guide to Being a Sex Goddess*. New York: Penguin Group, 2004.

Cunningham, Scott. *Cunningham's Encyclopedia of Crystal, Gem & Metal Magic*. St. Paul, MN: Llewellyn, 1992.

————. *Earth, Air, Fire & Water: More Techniques of Natural Magic*. St. Paul, MN: Llewellyn, 1992.

————. *Magical Aromatherapy*. St. Paul, MN: Llewellyn, 1993.

Curott, Phyllis. *The Love Spell*. New York: Gotham Books, 2005.

Day, Laura. *Practical Intuition in Love*. New York: HarperCollins, 1998.

Dolnick, Barrie. *Simple Spells for Love*. New York: Harmony Books, 1995.

Dolnick, Barrie, Julia Condon, and Donna Limoges. *Sexual Bewitchery and Other Ancient Feminine Wiles*. New York: Avon Books, 1998.

Dugan, Ellen. *Cottage Witchery*. St. Paul, MN: Llewellyn, 2005.

———. *Elements of Witchcraft: Natural Magick for Teens*. St. Paul, MN: Llewellyn, 2003.

———. *The Enchanted Cat*. Woodbury, MN: Llewellyn, 2006.

———. *Garden Witchery*. St. Paul, MN: Llewellyn, 2003.

———. *Herb Magic for Beginners*. Woodbury, MN: Llewellyn, 2006.

———. "June." *The 2008 Llewellyn Witches' Calendar*. Woodbury, MN: Llewellyn, 2007.

———. *7 Days of Magic*. St. Paul, MN: Llewellyn, 2004.

Dunwich, Gerina. *The Magick of Candle Burning*. New York: Citadel Press, 1989.

Gallagher, Ann-Marie. *The Spells Bible*. Cincinnati, OH: Walking Stick Press, 2003.

Gillotte, Galen. *Sacred Stones of the Goddess*. St. Paul, MN: Llewellyn, 2003.

Illes, Judika. *The Element Encyclopedia of 5,000 Spells*. New York: Element, 2004.

Johnson, Anna. *Three Black Skirts*. New York: Workman Publishing Company, 2000.

Lapanja, Margie. *The Goddess' Guide to Love*. Berkeley, CA: Conari Press, 1999.

Laufer, Geraldine Adamich. *Tussie-Mussies: The Language of Flowers*. New York: Workman Publishing Company, 1993.

McCoy, Edain. *If You Want to Be a Witch*. St. Paul, MN: Llewellyn, 2004.

McLelland, Lilith. *The Salem Witches' Book of Love Spells*. New York: Citadel Press, 1998.

Medici, Marina. *Good Magic*. New York: Simon & Schuster, 1992.

Morrison, Dorothy. *Enchantments of the Heart*. Franklin Lakes, NJ: New Page Books, 2002.

Nahmad, Claire. *Earth Magic: A Wisewoman's Guide to Herbal, Astrological & Other Folk Wisdom*. Rochester, VT: Destiny Books, 1994.

Penczak, Christopher. *The Outer Temple of Witchcraft*. St. Paul, MN: Llewellyn, 2004.

———. *The Shamanic Temple of Witchcraft*. St. Paul, MN: Llewellyn, 2005.

Ravenwolf, Silver. *Silver's Spells for Love*. St. Paul, MN: Llewellyn, 2001.

Rich, Ronda. *What Southern Women Know About Flirting*. New York: Penguin Group, 2005.

Skolnick, Solomon M. *The Language of Flowers*. White Plains, NY: Peter Pauper Press, 1995.

Sylvan, Dianne. *The Body Sacred*. Woodbury, MN: Llewellyn, 2005.

Telesco, Patricia. *Goddess in My Pocket*. New York: HarperCollins, 1998.

———. *A Little Book of Love Magic*. Freedom, CA: Crossing Press, 1999.

Trobe, Kala. *Invoke the Goddess*. St. Paul, MN: Llewellyn, 2000.

————. *The Witch's Guide to Life*. St. Paul, MN: Llewellyn, 2003.

Williamson, Marianne. *Enchanted Love*. New York: Simon & Schuster, 1999.

Websites

www.victorianhalloween.com: Victorian Halloween info (accessed 11/7/2007)

www.thecompletevictorian.homestead.com/halloween.html: Victorian Halloween info (accessed 11/7/2007)

www.romantic-lyrics.com/flirtideas.shtml: Flirting tips (accessed 11/7/2007)

http://en.wikipedia.org/wiki/Perfumes: Categories of perfume scents (accessed 11/7/2007)

http://www.beautybuzz.com/scent.asp?page=families: "Fragrance Families" by Denise Petals (accessed 11/7/2007)

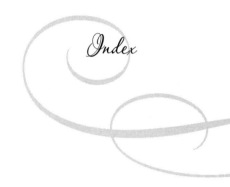

Index

index

♥

index

Free Catalog

Get the latest information on
our body, mind, and spirit products!
To receive a **free** copy of Llewellyn's consumer
catalog, *New Worlds of Mind & Spirit,* simply call
1-877-NEW-WRLD or visit our website at
www.llewellyn.com and click on *New Worlds.*

LLEWELLYN ORDERING INFORMATION

 Order Online:
Visit our website at www.llewellyn.com, select your books, and order them on our
secure server.

 Order by Phone:
- Call toll-free within the U.S. at 1-877-NEW-WRLD
  (1-877-639-9753). Call toll-free within Canada at
  1-866-NEW-WRLD (1-866-639-9753)
- We accept VISA, MasterCard, and American Express

 Order by Mail:
Send the full price of your order (MN residents add 6.5% sales tax) in
U.S. funds, plus postage & handling to:

Llewellyn Worldwide
2143 Wooddale Drive, Dept. 978-0-7387-1113-3
Woodbury, MN 55125-2989

Postage & Handling:

Standard (U.S., Mexico & Canada). If your order is:
 $24.99 and under, add $3.00
 $25.00 and over, FREE STANDARD SHIPPING

AK, HI, PR: $15.00 for one book plus $1.00 for
each additional book.

International Orders (airmail only):
 $16.00 for one book plus $3.00 for each additional book

Orders are processed within 2 business days.
Please allow for normal shipping time. Postage and handling rates subject to change.

Garden Witchery
Magick from the Ground Up
(Includes a Gardening Journal)

Ellen Dugan

How Does Your Magickal Garden Grow?

Garden Witchery is more than belladonna and wolfsbane. It's about making your own enchanted backyard with the trees, flowers, and plants found growing around you. It's about creating your own flower fascinations and spells, and it's full of common-sense information about cold hardiness zones, soil requirements, and a realistic listing of accessible magickal plants.

There may be other books on magickal gardening, but none have practical gardening advice, magickal correspondences, flower folklore, moon gardening, faerie magick, advanced Witchcraft, and humorous personal anecdotes all rolled into one volume.

978-0-7387-0318-3
272 pp., 7½ x 7½ $16.95

7 Days of Magic
Spells, Charms & Correspondences
for the Bewitching Week

Ellen Dugan

Every Day Is a Bewitching Day

Enchantment is not limited to the sabbats and the occasional full moon. Magic happens all the time and every day, and *7 Days of Magic* demonstrates how to successfully apply the specific magical energies of each day into spells, charms, and rituals.

Forget about memorizing massive correspondence charts. This practical, easy-to-use guide encourages readers to learn at their own pace. Every chapter—one for each day of the week—contains a small table of magical correspondences (planetary influence and symbol, deities, flowers and plants, metals, colors, crystals and stones, tarot cards, herbs and spices), which are talked about in-depth within seven distinct sections. Each chapter ends with a magical potpourri of sample spells and rituals.

978-0-7387-0589-7
240 pp., 7½ x 7½   **$12.95**

Cottage Witchery
Natural Magick for
Hearth and Home

Ellen Dugan

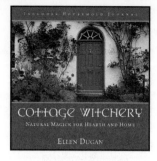

There's no place like a magickal home, and Ellen Dugan, the author of *Garden Witchery*, is the ideal guide to show us how to bring the beauty of nature and its magickal energies indoors. Using common household and outdoor items—such as herbs, spices, dried flowers, plants, stones, and candles—she offers a down-to-earth approach to creating an enchanted home.

From specialized spells and charms to kitchen conjuring and color magick, this hands-on guide teaches Witches of all levels how to strengthen a home's aura and energy. Readers will learn how to use begonias and lilacs for protection, dispel bad vibes with salt and lemon, perform tea leaf readings, bless the home with fruit, invite the help of faeries, perform houseplant magick, and create a loving home for the whole family.

978-0-7387-0625-2
288 pp., 7½ x 7½   **$16.95**

to order, call 1-877-new-wrld
Prices subject to change without notice

Elements of Witchcraft
Natural Magick for Teens

Ellen Dugan

This is a teen primer on the theory, techniques, and tools of natural magick.

Being a witch is not just about casting spells. It's also about magick—the magick of nature and of life. This book, by a veteran witch and mother of three teenagers, shows teens how natural magick is both quietly beautiful and unstoppably powerful, and how they can harness that energy to better their own lives.

The young seeker will be introduced to the theory of witchcraft, the God and the Goddess, and ethical considerations. There are elemental meditations, correspondence charts, nature spirit information, magickal herbalism, spells, and charms. Teens will also learn how to create their own magickal tools and altars with natural supplies, cast a circle, avoid magickal mistakes, and live a magickal life.

978-0-7387-0393-0
288 pp., 6 x 9, illus.   **$14.95**

Autumn Equinox
The Enchantment of Mabon

Ellen Dugan

Mabon, Feast of Avalon, Cornucopia, Harvest Home, Festival of the Vine ... there are many names for this magickal holiday that celebrates the autumn equinox, the first day of fall. Ellen Dugan takes a fresh look at this "forgotten" sabbat and demonstrates how to make the most of this enchanting season.

Featuring craft projects, recipes, enchantments, and valuable information on harvest deities, *Autumn Equinox* offers countless ways to bring fall magick into your life. Learn to create witchy wreaths, cook seasonal foods, put together a homemade centerpiece, make herbal soap, and practice spells and rituals using natural, easy-to-find supplies. Part of Llewellyn's Sabbats series, this book also provides magickal correspondences on harvest deities, herbs, plants, and foods for those who want to create their own autumn spells and charms.

978-0-7387-0624-5
240 pp., 7 ½ x 9 ⅛
$14.95

to order, call 1-877-new-wrld
Prices subject to change without notice

The Enchanted Cat
Feline Fascinations, Spells & Magick
Ellen Dugan

From the temples of ancient Egypt to the homes of modern Witches, cats have long been associated with magick and mystery. Examining cat mythology and folklore from around the world and sprinkled with enchanting cat quotes from famous feline admirers throughout the ages, *The Enchanted Cat* is a must-read for any magickal cat fancier.

Witches, Pagans, and other magick-minded folks will love the dozens of charms, spells, and meditations included for working with feline power. A naming ceremony, lists of magickal cat names and correspondences, and spells and charms for your cat's collar are just a sampling of the feline-friendly magick inside. Cat astrology, tarot, and even a discussion of feline feng shui make *The Enchanted Cat* a uniquely magickal exploration of our enduring fascination with the feline mystique.

978-0-7387-0769-3
192 pp., 7½ x 7½   **$12.95**

Herb Magic for Beginners
Down-to-Earth Enchantments

Ellen Dugan

Stir up passion with violet or nab a new job with honeysuckle. From parsley to periwinkle, people enjoy herbs for their aroma, taste, and healing abilities, but few are aware of the enchanting powers harnessed within these multipurpose plants. Breathing new life into herbal folklore and wisdom, Ellen Dugan introduces the magical side of these natural treasures.

The author of *Cottage Witchery* describes the magical traits of flowers, roots, trees, spices, and other commonly found herbs. Under her guidance, readers learn the basics of magic and spellworking so they may safely explore herbal magic on their own for health, luck, prosperity, romance, protection, and more!

978-0-7387-0837-9
216 pp., 5¾₁₆ x 8 $12.95

Also available in Spanish as *Magia con las hierbas*

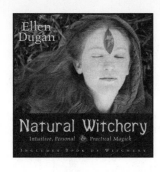

Natural Witchery
Intuitive, Personal & Practical Magick

Ellen Dugan

Natural Witchery offers dozens of ways to hone your intuition, enhance your magickal powers, and enliven your everyday practice.

Ellen Dugan goes to the heart of what it means to be a natural Witch. Forget about lineage, degrees, and politically correct titles. Her thoughtful observations and wise words will guide you back to what's important: forging your own unique spiritual path. These engaging exercises will help you look within yourself and stretch your psychic talents, discover your elemental strengths, and charge up your personal power.

Dugan's personal anecdotes and humor liven up the lessons and keep you grounded throughout the daily joys and trials of life as a natural Witch.

978-0-7387-0922-2
288 pp., 7½ x 7½   **$16.95**

To Write to the Author

If you wish to contact the author or would like more information about this book, please write to the author in care of Llewellyn Worldwide and we will forward your request. Both the author and publisher appreciate hearing from you and learning of your enjoyment of this book and how it has helped you. Llewellyn Worldwide cannot guarantee that every letter written to the author can be answered, but all will be forwarded. Please write to:

Ellen Dugan
℅ Llewellyn Worldwide
2143 Wooddale Drive, Dept. 978-0-7387-1113-3
Woodbury, MN 55125-2989

Please enclose a self-addressed stamped envelope for reply,
or $1.00 to cover costs. If outside U.S.A., enclose
international postal reply coupon.

Many of Llewellyn's authors have websites with additional information and resources. For more information, please visit our website:

HTTP://WWW.LLEWELLYN.COM